This book is dedicated to the memory of General George Armstrong Custer and to the photographers of his period. It is dedicated as well to the giants of fine art photography, my friends and mentors George R. Rinhart and the late Lloyd Ostendorf. Their friendship, guidance and support brought me to a place they alone understand.

To my wonderful children, Shaun and Brianne

The publisher wishes to extend a personal thank you to the following Friends of the Museum: Mr. and Mrs. Brad Spear; Mr. & Mrs. Paul Harbaugh; Charles "Timer" Moses, Esq.; Harold Stanton, Esq.; Rhonda Elhard; Tyler Baldwin; Mr. and Mrs. David Miller; Mr. and Mrs. Paul Miller; Robert Garritson; Mr. and Mrs. James Thompson; Thomas Minckler, Thomas Waugh; Richard Ioset, Esq.; Congressman Dennis Rehberg (R-MT); U.S. Senator Conrad Burns (R-MT); my son Clinton Kortlander and the United States Supreme Court.

Major General George Armstrong Custer being photographed by Alexander Gardner. From the original ink wash by Lloyd Ostendorf in the author's collection.

CUSTER
IN PHOTOGRAPHS

by

D. Mark Katz

Custer Battlefield Museum Publishing

Garryowen, Montana

www.custermuseum.org

White Bull and General Godfrey "bury the hatchet" at the 50th Anniversary, 1926 inside the tomb of the unknown soldier at Garryowen.   Photo by Elsa Spear Byron

Published by
CUSTER BATTLEFIELD MUSEUM
GARRYOWEN, MONTANA

General George Armstrong Custer's last moments on Earth were so memorable that today – 125 years later – nearly 500,000 visitors make the annual pilgrimage to the historic site which marks his demise. Because of this, the Little Big Horn Battlefield is one the most recognized military sites in the world.

Today, the small township of Garryowen, Montana is located on the spot that marks the first skirmish of the Battle of the Little Big Horn, yet despite the one hundred and twenty-five years that have passed from that moment to this, the banks of the Little Big Horn River would still look familiar to Custer if he were to return today.

Garryowen is also the location of the Custer Battlefield Museum, site of the new Peace Monument unveiled on June 24th, 2001 – the 125th Anniversary of the Battle of the Little Big Horn. It is located adjacent to the Tomb of the Unknown Soldier, believed to be one of the first men to die in the battle.

The *Peace Monument* reads:

"When we stand side by side in the circle of no beginning and no ending,
the first maker, creator of all things, is in the center.
He hears our words of supplication and blesses us
With his infinite love, which is 'Peace' itself."

Joe Medicine Crow, Ph.D
"High Bird" – Dagak Bako
Crow Tribal Historian
Grandson of Custer's Last Scout,
White Man Runs Him

All profits from the sale of this publication will go toward maintaining and expanding the Museum's collections, as well as toward the preservation and upkeep of the Peace Monument and the Tomb of the Unknown Soldier, located in historic Garryowen, Montana. My vision to found the nonprofit Custer Battlefield Museum was realized in 1995. Donations of all kind are tax deductible and used to promote historic conservation and public education.

Christopher Kortlander, Director
Custer Battlefield Museum

"A tragedy that no one won. A battle, all parties lost."

Joe Medicine Crow, Ph.D

Son of The Morning Star was the name given to George Custer by his Crow Indian scouts. It was descriptive as well as a prophetic way of calling this pony soldier chief.

The Crow scouts regarded his appearance as impressive-tall and colorful, with the brilliance of the morning star (Venus) itself as it glitters in the early morning sky.

Here on earth he is the human being son of the celestial star;
in future time his name will always shine and be remembered forever and ever!

Here is a Crow Indian Honor Song for Son Of The Morning Star
Composed by Joseph Medicine Crow, a grandson of General Custer's favorite and last scout:

> Will every one look at me,
> I am Son Of the Morning Star.
> Look at me and remember me.
>
> Will every one look at me.
> I am a Pony Soldier Chief.
> Look at me and remember me.
>
> Will every one look at me.
> I fought at the Little Big Horn.
> Remember me always.
>
> Will every one look at me.
> I fought the mighty Sioux and Cheyenne,
> Remember me always and always.

"Custer in Photographs" is a pictorial historical record, as was also expressed by his Crow Scouts in song. The Crows thought the world of him. That is the reason they gave him the powerful name, "Son of the Morning Star". He was told, "Too many Sioux" and he knew it. He was very determined, they considered him very brave.

Joe Medicine Crow, Ph.D
High Bird- Dagak Bako
Crow Tribal Historian
Grandson of Custer's Last Scout Whiteman Runs Him & Chief Medicine Crow

Copyright © 2001 by D. Mark Katz
All rights reserved.

This 2001 special edition is limited to 2000 copies. Published by Custer Battlefield Museum Publishing, distributed by Historical Rarities, Inc., P.O. Box 200, Town Hall, Garryowen, MT 59031, 406.638.2020 www.historicalrarities.com by arrangement with the author.

Printed and bound in USA. All rights reserved. No part of this book may be reproduced in any form or by any electronic or mechanical means including information storage and retrieval systems without permission in writing from the publisher, except by a reviewer, who may quote brief passages in a review.

Printed and bound by Artcraft Printers, Billings, Montana

Library of Congress Cataloging-in-Publication Data
Katz, D. Mark
    Custer in Photographs / by D. Mark Katz
    Reprint. Originally published: Gettysburg, PA: Yo-Mark
Production Co., © 1985
ISBN 0-517-02745-3
1. Custer, George Armstrong. 1839-1876 - Pictorial Works.
2. Generals - United States - Pictorial Works. 1. Title.

Third Edition, Hardcover ISBN 0-9711881-1-4
Third Edition, Softcover ISBN 0-9711881-0-6

A deluxe limited edition of 125 copies, enclosed in slip case, featuring an original photograph of General George Armstrong Custer and autographed by the author, Director of the Custer Battlefield Museum and Dr. Joe Medicine Crow is available.

CASUALTIES OF THE BATTLE OF THE LITTLE BIG HORN

7TH CAVALRY HEADQUARTERS STAFF

- Lt. Col. George Armstrong Custer
- 1st Lieutenant William Winer Cooke
- Sergeant Major William H. Sharrow
- Chief Trumpeter Henry Voss

ATTACHED

- Assistant Surgeon George E. Lord
- Acting Assistant Surgeon James M. DeWolf

COMPANY A

- 1ST Sergeant William Heyn
- Corporal James Dalious
- Corporal George H. King
- Private John E. Armstrong
- Private James Drinan
- Private James McDonald
- Private William Moodie
- Private Richard Rollins
- Private John Sullivan
- Private Thomas P. Sweetzer

COMPANY B

- 2ND Lt. Benjamin H. Hodgson
- Private Richard B. Dorn
- Private George B. Mask

COMPANY C

- Capt. Thomas Ward Custer
- 2nd Lt. Henry Moore Harrington
- 1st Sgt. L. Edwin Bobo
- Sgt. George Finckle
- Sgt. Jeremiah Finley
- Corporal Henry E. French
- Corporal Daniel Ryan
- Trumpeter Thomas J. Bucknell
- Trumpeter William Kramer
- Blacksmith John King
- Saddler George Howell
- Private Fred E. Allan
- Private James Bennett
- Private John Brightfield
- Private Christopher Criddle
- Private George Eiseman
- Private Gustave Engle
- Private James Farrand
- Private Patrick Giffin
- Private James Hathersall
- Private John Lewis
- Private August Meyer
- Private Edgar Phillips
- Private John Rauter
- Private Edward Rix
- Private James H. Russell
- Private Samuel S. Shade
- Private Jeremiah Shea
- Private Nathan Short
- Private Ludwick St. John
- Private Alpheus Stuart
- Private Ygnatz Stungewitz
- Private Thadus
- Private Garrett W. Van Allen
- Private Oscar T. Warner
- Private Henry Wyman

COMPANY D

- Farrier Vincent Charley
- Private Patrick M. Golden
- Private Edward Housen

COMPANY E

- 1st Lt. Algernon E. Smith
- 2ND Lt. James Garland Sturgis
- 1st Sgt. Frederick Hohmeyer
- Sgt. William B. James
- Sgt. John S. Ogden
- Corporal George C. Brown
- Corporal Thomas P. Eagan
- Corporal Albert H. Meyer
- Trumpeter Thomas McElroy
- Trumpeter George A. Moonie
- Private William H. Baker
- Private Robert Barth
- Private Owen Boyle
- Private James Brogan
- Private Edward Connor
- Private John Darris
- Private William Davis
- Private Richard Farrell
- Private John S.S. Forbes
- Private John Heim
- Private John Henderson
- Private Sykes Henderson
- Private William Huber
- Private Andrew Knecht
- Private Herod T. Liddiard
- Private Patrick E. O'Connor
- Private William H. Rees
- Private Edward Rood

Company E (Continued):

- Private Henry Schele
- Private William Smallwood
- Private Albert A. Smith
- Private James Smith [1]
- Private James Smith [2]
- Private Benjamin F. Stafford
- Private Alexander Stella
- Private William A. Torrey
- Private Cornelius Van Sant
- Private George P. Walker

COMPANY F

- Capt. George W. M. Yates
- 2nd Lt. William Van Wyck Reily
- 1st Sgt. Michael Kenney
- Sgt. John H. Groesbeck
- Sgt. Frederick Nursey
- Sgt. John R. Wilkinson
- Corporal John Briody
- Corporal Charles Coleman
- Corporal William Teeman
- Trumpeter Thomas N. Way
- Farrier Benjamin Brandon
- Blacksmith James R. Manning
- Private Thomas Atcheson
- Private William Brady
- Private Benjamin F. Brown
- Private Patrick Bruce
- Private Lucien Burnham
- Private James Carney
- Private Armantheus D. Cather
- Private Timothy Donnelly
- Private John Gardner
- Private George W. Hammon

- Private John P. Kelly
- Private Gustav Klein
- Private Herman Knauth
- Private William H. Lerock
- Private Werner L. Liemann
- Private William A. Lossee
- Private Christian Madsen
- Private Francis E. Milton
- Private Joseph Monroe
- Private Sebastian Omling
- Private Patrick Rudden
- Private Richard D. Saunders
- Private Francis W. Sicfous
- Private George A. Warren

COMPANY G

- 1ST Lt. Donald McIntosh
- Sgt. Edward Botzer
- Sgt. Martin Considine
- Corporal Otto Hagemann
- Trumpeter Henry C. Dose (Custer Battalion)
- Farrier Benjamin O. Wells
- Saddler Crawford Selby
- Private John J. McGinniss
- Private Andrew J. Moore
- Private John Rapp
- Private Benjamin F. Rogers
- Private Henry Seafferman
- Private Edward Stanley

COMPANY H

- Corporal George Lell
- Private Henry Black
- Private William M. George
- Private Private Julien D. Jones
- Private Thomas Meador

COMPANY I

- Capt. Myles Walter Keogh
- 1st Lt. James Ezekiel Porter
- 1st Sgt. Frank E. Varden
- Sgt. James Bustard
- Corporal George C. Morris
- Corporal Samuel F. Staples
- Corporal John Wild
- Trumpeter John McGucker
- Trumpeter John W. Patton

- Blacksmith Henry A. Bailey
- Private John D. Barry
- Private Joseph F. Broadhurst
- Private Thomas Connors
- Private David Cooney
- Private Thomas Downing
- Private Edward C. Driscoll
- Private David C. Gillette
- Private George H. Gross
- Private Adam Hetesimer
- Private Edward P. holcomb
- Private Marion Horn
- Private Patrick Kelly
- Private Frederick Lehman
- Private Henry Lehmann
- Private Edward W. Loyd
- Private Archibald McIlhargey
- Private John E. Mitchell
- Private Jacob Noshang
- Private John O'Bryan
- Private John Parker
- Private Felix Pitter
- Private George Post
- Private James Quinn
- Private William Reed
- Private John W. Rossbury
- Private Darwin L. Symms
- Private James E. Troy
- Private Charles Van Bramer
- Private William B. Whaley

COMPANY K

- 1st Sgt. DeWitt Winney
- Sgt. Robert H. Hughes
- Corporal John J. Callahan
- Trumpeter Julius Helmer
- Private Elihu F. Clear

COMPANY L

- 1ST Lt. James Calhoun
- 2nd Lt. John Jordan Crittenden
- 1st Sgt. James Butler
- Sgt. William Cashan
- Sgt. Amos B. Warren
- Corporal William H. Gilbert
- Corporal William H. Harrison
- Corporal John Seiler
- Trumpeter Frederick Walsh
- Farrier William H. Heath
- Blacksmith Charles Siemon

- Saddler Charles Perkins
- Private George E. Adams
- Private William Andrews
- Private Anthony Assadaly
- Private Elmer Babcock
- Private Ami Cheever
- Private William B. Crisfield
- Private John L. Crowley
- Private William Dye
- Private James J. Galvan
- Private Charles Graham
- Private Henry Hamilton
- Private Weston Harrington
- Private Louis Hauggi
- Private Francis T. Hughes
- Private Thomas G. Kavanagh
- Private Louis Lobering
- Private Bartholomew Mahoney
- Private Thomas E. Maxwell
- Private Charles McCarthy
- Private Peter McGue
- Private John Miller
- Private David J. O'Connell
- Private Oscar F. Pardee
- Private Christian Reibold
- Private Walter B. Rogers
- Private Charles Schmidt
- Private Charles Scott
- Private Bent Siemonson
- Private Andrew Snow
- Private Byron L. Tarbox
- Private Edmund D. Tessier
- Private Thomas S. Tweed
- Private M.Vetter

COMPANY M

- Sgt. Miles F. O'Hara
- Corporal Henry M. Cody
- Corporal Frederick Stressinger
- Private Frank Braun
- Private Jacob H. Gebhart
- Private Henry Gordon
- Private Henry Klotzbucher
- Private George Lorentz
- Private William D. Meyer
- Private George E. Smith
- Private David Summers
- Private Henry Turley
- Private Henry C. Voight

U.S. Indian Scouts & Guides

- Guide/Interpreter Bloody Knife
- U.S. Indian Scout Bob Tailed Bull
- U.S. Indian Scout Little Brave

U.S. Quartermaster Department Employees & Citizens

- Mitch Bouyer, Interpreter
- Boston Custer, Guide
- Harry Armstrong Reed, Beef Herder
- Isaiah Dorman, Interpreter
- Charles Alexander Reynolds, Guide
- Marcus Henry Kellog, Attached Correspondent

CHEYENNE

Southern Cheyenne

- Chief Lame White Man

Northern Cheyenne

- Black Bear
- Black Cloud
- Black Coyote
- Flying By
- Full Beard
- Owns Red Horse
- Hump Nose
- Left Hand
- Noisy Walking
- Little Whirlwind
- Cut Belly
- Closed hand
- Swift Cloud
- Limber Bones
- Roman Nose
- Old Man
- Hair Lip
- Young Bear
- An Unknown Woman

LAKOTA SIOUX

Hunkpapa:

- War Leader Chief Black Moon
- Hawk Man
- Guts
- Red Face
- White Bull
- Bear With Horns
- Gall's two Wives
- Gall's three daughters

Minneconjou:

- Dog's Backbone
- Dog With Horns
- Three Bears
- Swift Bear
- High Horse

Oglala:

- Bad Light Hair
- Plenty Lice
- White Eagle
- Young Skunk
- Black Wasichu
- Elk Stands On Top

Sans Arc:

- Elk Bear
- Cloud Man
- Deed
- Kills Him
- Long Dog
- Chief Elk Standing High
- Long Road (Also Known as Long Robe)
- Eagle Hat
- Two Bear
- Two Kettle
- Chased By Owls

Blackfeet:

- Flying Charge

Band Not Known

- Black Fox
- Flying By (Band?)
- Young Black Moon (Band?)
- Chief High Eagle (Band?)
- White Buffalo Bull (Band?)
- Mustache (Band?)
- Young Bear

Acknowledgments

This 125th Special Anniversary Commemoration Edition would not have been possible without the cooperation, vision and support of Mr. Christopher Kortlander, director of the Custer Battlefield Museum, and their Board of Directors, James "Putt" Thompson, Curator and Pius Real Bird.

This project could not have been achieved without the help and support of a certain few individuals whose faith led them not only to contribute their time and efforts, but their friendship, support and loyalty as well.

A major contribution was made by Neil Mangum, Superintendent and John Doehner, historian for the Little Big Horn National Monument. These two individuals provided me original photographs from the Elizabeth B. Custer Collection housed at the Battlefield, and allowed me the opportunity to copy directly from their original images.

I salute Brian Pohanka for his tremendous knowledge and eye for detail. Without his expertise, most of the identifications, both dates and descriptions could not have been accurately cited. Through Brian's scholarly research, I was provided with information that led to the location and identification of new material.

William A. Frassanito, the acknowledged expert on Civil War Photography played a crucial role in the final stages of publication. His unselfish commitment to this project allowed me to see it through to its completion.

A certain group of individuals went way beyond the realm of expectation, affording me the opportunity to copy original images from their private collections. These generous friends were: Dr. Lawrence A. Frost; Dale Anderson; Darryl Lyons; Karl Rommel; Wilfred Thompson; Lloyd Ostendorf; David Hack; Craig Haffner; Stephanie Lower; William A. Frassanito; Joe Gustin; Keya Mazhari; Arthur C. Unger and George R. Rinhart.

The following institutions graciously responded to my request for their material on George A. Custer: Amon Carter Museum; South 'Dakota Historical Society; The Maryland Historical Society; Burton Historical Collection of the Detroit Public Library; California Historical Society; Brigham Young University; Colorado Historical Society; University of Oklahoma at Norman; Nebraska State Historical Society; The Western Reserve Historical Society; The Society of California Pioneers; The National Hall of Fame for Famous American Indians; Chicago Public Library; The Bentley Historical Library of the University of Michigan; North Dakota Parks and Recreation Department; Utah State Historical Society; George Eastman House; Buffalo Bill Museum; Fort Larned National Historic Site; The Historical Society of Pennsylvania; University of California at Los Angeles; Idaho State Historical Society; Missouri Historical Society; Texas State Library; Wyoming State Archives; Custer State Park; State Historical Society of Wisconsin; Fort Laramie National Historic Site; Chicago Historical Society; State Archives of the Michigan Historical Division; Sternberg Memorial Museum and The Western Reserve Historical Society.

The following institutions provided material for the book: Little Big Horn National Monument; The Library of Congress, with special thanks to its helpful staff, Jerold Maddox, Carol Johnson, Meja Felaco and Mary Ison who authorized the use of its original negatives. The National Archives, which also allowed me to use its original negatives; South Dakota Historical Society, which provided me with a contact print from one of its original negatives taken during the Black Hills Expedition; Harrison County Historical Society; The National Portrait Gallery, Smithsonian Institution; New York Public Library; United States Army Military History Institute; United States Military Academy, West Point, both the Library and the Department of Special Collections; Eugene Ostroff at the Department of Photography, American History Institute, who provided me with two contact prints from the Museum's original negatives; The Beinecke Rare Book and Manuscript Library, Yale University; The Monroe County Historical Commission; Kansas State Historical Society; the State Historical Society of North Dakota and the Henry E. Huntington Library and Art Gallery.

The following technical consultants shared their expertise, knowledge and resources: Barry Lipschutz who guided me all the way during the initial printing - a friend who went beyond the realm of his job imparting consideration and expert advice. Bill Benson, who introduced me to the quality of duotone printing; Walt Lane who provided me with excellent copy negatives and Dennis Tresidder and Donna Keller of Artcraft Printers who worked tirelessly with Christopher Kortlander and the author on improving the first edition, thanks.

Finally, there are those who offered me the inspiration and encouragement necessary to complete this sometimes arduous task. I especially thank William A. Frassanito; the late Lloyd Ostendorf; Dr. Roland Bill; Tom Budnick; the late Roy Meredith; Julie Landis; Frank Mercantante; Jim Shea; Nick Picerno; Brian Pohanka; Charles Wallace; Mary Ford and to my good friends David Hack; Frank DiMauro; George Rinhart, Bud and Patsy Gatlin, Craig Haffner, Jack and Mary Rose Torres and David and JK Mulberg.

Preface

History has a way of bestowing a more lasting immortality on important people who die at the height of their earthly achievements. Famous personalties who are cut down at the height of their fame leave people clamoring to know more about them. Books and songs are written about them. Pictorial mementoes and keepsakes are in demand.

The celebrated military figure General George Armstrong Custer, whose life ended so abruptly, is no exception. Interest in him has never diminished with the passing of time.

It seems fitting that a serious effort to collect and evaluate a complete visual study of Custer's photographs has been achieved. In a labor of love, Mark Katz has succeeded in searching out and cataloging the great number of Custer images in existence. From museums, collectors, family and archival sources, come an impressive compilation. So many Custer photographs have come to light after a diligent search that the number of likenesses now exceeds the number of known photographs taken of Abraham Lincoln — once thought to be the most photographed man of his time.

This volume contains the most complete collection of Custer photographs ever assembled. Many Custer camera studies are reproduced here for the first time. Little-known and unpublished portraits of the legendary general reveal fresh insights into his appearance that have long been overlooked or never known to have existed. All these old photos form an exciting and significant parade of pictures, a chronology of this American hero from youth to his untimely death.

The author's numerical order and arrangement are essential to properly catalog the many Custer images for historians and posterity. From these picture-pages emerge the finest and most definitive compilation of Custer photographs every likely to be assembled.

The pictures of Custer reveal an ever-changing appearance in the man's features — his yellow hair in different styles and length; his strong lean face, befreckled and adorned by whiskered variations, all adequately caught by his contemporary cameramen.

It may be safe to say there were hardly any more colorful characters in American history than Custer. By the same token, there could hardly have been any more captivating pictures taken than those of this man, thick in the epic of the Civil War and Indian Wars.

This youthful and dashing military figure becomes the most photogenic personality known to early photography. Along with the images of his pretty wife and associates, it is all the more reason his pictures should be commemorated in this book.

Everyone loves a winner, and Custer, a man of action, gained his share of military victories and the admiration of the contemporary press as well as the people.

That he was a rash and somewhat egotistical man seems evident. His unique military uniforms and western attire reveal his good taste in design. His proud and handsome features were a frequent subject before the cameras. His life in words and pictures tells of the wanderlust in his blood — his brash nature, the extent of which still carries over today. The 100,000 visitors to the Custer Memorial Battlefield each summer attest to the worship of his winsome ways. The current increasing prices realized for his images and artifacts further signify his popularity with collectors and admirers.

The power and myths of the Custer story attract the public's fancy. He holds an exceptional position in history, that of a "double-barreled" hero. He was not only a flamboyant Civil War notable, but also an outstanding figure in the winning of the Old West.

Whether considered brave or foolhardy in his military exploits, his conquests cannot be overlooked. His pictures add drama to the story of his life. And the shadows of his many photographs taken before his dramatic end give us an enduring departed soldier — one whose image will never fade away.

Of the cameraman's contribution to Custer's immortality, their lenses focused on him often, yet he was never daguerreotyped. Ten original tintypes and four ambrotypes from life exist. Over 24 cabinet-size photographs and eight stereoscopic card photos add to the impressive number. Also skillfully reproduced in this fine volume are 46 direct contact albumen prints. A dozen imperial photographs from the large glass negatives are reproduced, all printed with such fidelity that they seem to show an added dimension.

This monumental and plausible effort compromises a total of Custer poses in excess of 150 pictures, 71 of which are taken with others or in group scenes. Perhaps someday more Custer photos will be found, but this is a definitive work—a visual inspiration—that will not easily be challenged.

Lloyd Ostendorf

Foreword

George Armstrong Custer was without question one of the most colorful and intriguing American military figures to emerge during the second half of the nineteenth century. His prominent role in numerous engagements of the Civil War — at Gettysburg, Yellow Tavern, Winchester, and Five Forks; and later during the Indian Wars on the battlefields of the Washita River and the Little Big Horn — made him a legend in his own time. Today, more than a century later, the legend persists, enhanced several-fold by the passage of time and the ever-growing remoteness of an age when horse-mounted warriors thundered across the open plains of the American frontier.

The Custer story is well-known, and although the "ultimate" history of the man, his life and death, will never be written, myriad aspects of his career already have been researched and chronicled many times over, the resulting books and articles being readily accessible to historians and students alike.

This volume, *Custer In Photographs*, is by no means intended to recount once again the verbal story of Custer's life. It is rather, as its title implies, the first systematic attempt to gather, organize in an intelligent fashion, and analyze virtually every known photograph ever recorded of the man behind the legend. Few faces from our common past are as instantly recognizable as Custer's, and yet it is not generally known — as this study indicates so clearly, that Custer may well have been one of the most, if not the most photographed personage of his time. The number and variety of portraits reproduced in this volume are truly impressive.

Introduced to the world in 1839, photography existed and developed in various forms for a hundred years before its history came to be considered worthy of serious investigation by scholars whose backgrounds and sensitivity to non-verbal forms of communication adequately suited them to undertake the first sophisticated attempts at unraveling photography's past. Ironically, these initial, and now classic "general histories," have lulled many of the second generation of photographic historians into a complacency that accepts blindly and rehashes endlessly the same initial data, much of it now sadly outdated.

Fortunately there has surfaced in the last two decades an increasing number of photographic scholars who are breaking the psychological chains of past histories by delving into old, seemingly exhausted subject matter with a fresh and invigorating determination to distill hard data where once there was only vague and often inaccurate supposition. What the field of photographic history needs today are scores, indeed hundreds upon hundreds of in-depth micro-studies. We need to tackle countless topics referred to casually in the traditional general histories, and we need to dig into these topics as no one else has ever done before, until we have the names, the dates, the places, the unique circumstances — the hard data upon which valid conclusions must depend.

We owe a great debt to the first generation of photographic historians and their classic, often monumental studies. They have led the way. But the emphasis today must be on the exhaustive micro-history. And if we can accumulate enough of these finite investigations, perhaps in a decade or two we will be ready for another "History of Photography," but based the next time on a long overdue, and hopefully mountainous assemblage of heretofore unpublished data. The fresh documentation is out there, it just takes an enormous amount of energy to do the digging and the evaluation of evidence that is required.

Custer In Photographs is the result of just such an exhaustive endeavor. By gathering and studying every known photograph of George Armstrong Custer, Mark Katz has been able to shed fresh light on an outstanding example of how early cameramen handled one famous personage. The systematic and comprehensive nature of Katz's project has enabled him to garner connections, names, dates, etc. — items of documentation that will certainly add a significant building block to our expanding knowledge of photography's past. The future topics that await study are legion. We can only hope that the publication of *Custer In Photographs* will serve as a challenge and a guide in this pursuit of knowledge for many years to come.

William A. Frassanito
Gettysburg, Pa.

Introduction

Twenty years ago, I contemplated the notion of identifying and illustrating all the known photographs of George Armstrong Custer. If it were possible to locate one-hundred photographs, I knew that a book was realistic. I more than most, was pleased to identify 155 images, more than thirty percent being unpublished. Five years later, the second edition was published including three new views. It is fitting on this, the 125th Anniversary of Custer's final battle at the Little Big Horn, that this new edition is offered with four additional unknown views.

Custer today remains the most photographed man of the nineteenth century with 162 separate identifiable photographs spanning the last twenty years of his life. Interestingly enough, the photographs of George Armstrong Custer today remain the most valuable, many times eclipsing those of President Abraham Lincoln. If Custer in Photographs were published today for the first time, the value of each photograph might exceed twenty fold that from fifteen years ago when it was first published. It is safe to say that this project will span the rest of my life and that of my son Shaun, the keeper of the flame.

In June of 1857, young 17 year-old George Armstrong Custer decided to have his photographic portrait taken for the first time. The young lovestruck youth sat before the camera, rested his head ever so lightly on his right hand, while his arm rested on some books on the photographer's table. His hat was placed on his lap and just prior to the taking of the photograph, he held up an ambrotype portrait of his sweetheart, Mary Holland. A faint smile appeared on his lips and within five seconds, this moment was captured for all time. This frozen moment marked the beginning of a phenomenon, one which would continue throughout his short, yet illustrious life; for this would be the first known photographic sitting for a man who would become one of the most, if not the most photographed man of his time.

George Armstrong Custer had a tremendous love for life, family and the American dream. Rarely can one individual create such excitement and controversy within a single lifetime, regardless of its length. Yet George Custer did exactly that. He was a rambunctious youth, possessing unwavering courage. He had a tremendous responsibility thrust upon him at the tender age of twenty-four, when he became the youngest Major General in American history, a record which still stands. Indicative of the character of this noble warrior, this early responsibility and all other challenges were answered with honor. George Armstrong Custer, perhaps more than any other individual, helped create almost singlehandedly the mystique and tradition of the United States Cavalry which lives on today. During the Civil War he captured more armaments, more prisoners and more battle standards than any other commander, North or South, a record respected by his peers and acknowledged by his foes. He was a competent yet moderate agent for the United States Government in dealing with the Indians. And finally, he became a resolute martyr for the volatile Grant Administration while capturing the imagination of the entire nation.

The photographs in this book reveal a remarkable transformation which spans Custer's adult life from age seventeen through thirty-six.

Abraham Lincoln, the most photographed man of his time, had approximately 122 photographs taken of him. These photographs span nineteen years, from 1846 through his death in 1865. Custer sat for more than forty-two photographers on seventy-eight different occasions, accounting for 162 known photographs. Fifty-six photographs were published here for the first time. As a collector of Custer photographica, I was constantly amazed at the number of previously unknown Custer photographs that were being discovered. The main source of traditional photographic material seemed to be stockpiled at the Library of Congress, National Archives and the Little Big Horn National Monument. Since most published sources seemed to use the same photographs over and over, a vast quantity of rare material remained untapped. In 1964, the late Dr. Lawrence A. Frost published "The Custer Album, A Pictorial Biography of General George A. Custer." Although not intended to be the definitive photographic album, that work had until the publication of "Custer in Photographs" been considered the most complete collection of his images.

My objective in compiling this book was to first locate all the known photographs of George Custer. I then attempted to arrange the photographs in chronological order and to identify both the photograher and the original format of publication. For three years, I scoured the nation searching for Custer photographs, previously published poses, unpublished poses and all conceivable variations in each category. In many cases, I discovered that known yet obscure photographs had till now been overlooked when in fact they were actual significant unpublished variants. Along with the known repositories, hundreds of small and large historic societies and institutions were contacted. Most importantly, private collectors were solicited and in most instances were very cooperative. Hundreds of leads were followed and the entire country was traversed on numerous occasions in search of new and important portraits. I am not presumptuous enough to assert that all the photographs ever taken of Custer are herein illustrated, for I am realistically confident that others will surface in the future. Yet every effort has been made to assemble the most complete and comprehensive assemblage of Custer photographs ever amassed.

In order to assure faithful reproduction, all but a few of the duotones reproduced herein were copied directly from the original photograph in its original format. These portraits will be captioned "from the original." In many instances, a single photograph was published in different formats. When possible, the same photograph will be illustrated in its variant format, yet will maintain its common illustration number.

The photographs have been arranged in chronological order (a detailed chronology of Custer's life appears at the end of the book,) placing General Custer at a given location at a given time. In some instances where the date or place was uncertain, internal evidence was evaluated to approximate the photograph's placement within the chronology. For example, the length of Custer's hair was frequently an important source for dating the photographs. Custer was promoted to brigadier general on June 26, 1863. From June 1863, the sitting prior to his promotion, one will note that Custer's hair was relatively short. However, in September 1863, Custer's first portrait as brigadier general shows his hair to be shoulder length. Prior to his wedding on February 9th he cut his hair. This is evident in the portraits made on January 25, 1864. Then again on or about October 23 prior to the flag presentation ceremony his hair was cut again. This is shown in sketches of Custer in life made by Alfred Waud on October 9 with long hair and again on October 23 with short hair. During the progression of 1865, one will note the increased length of his hair. He did not cut his hair again until July in Hempstead, Texas. The only other time Custer's hair was long was in 1868 and again in 1873 prior to and during the Yellowstone Expedition.

To determine the identities of the photographers who actually recorded each view, it was necessary to examine the card mounts issued at the time of initial publication. In other instances, as in the case of those photographs published by David F. Barry, it is known that Orlando S. Goff was the original photographer and passed his negatives on to Barry in the 1880's. In the case of those portraits taken by Matthew Brady, one can assume that the portraits were made by an employee, not Brady himself. The artist will be identified as Matthew Brady & Co.

We will now open a window to the past and through the following pages study the strong, self-assured features of the last of the cavaliers, General George Armstrong Custer.

"I am not impetuous or impulsive. I resent that. Everything that I have ever done has been the result of the study that I have made of imaginary military situations that might arise. When I became engaged in campaign or battle and a great emergency arose, everything that I had ever read or studied focused in my mind as if the situation were under a magnifying glass and my decision was the instantaneous result. My mind worked instantaneously, but always as the result of everything I have ever studied being brought to bear on the situation."

George Armstrong Custer

Official service record of General George A. Custer:

He was a cadet at the United States Military Academy from July 1, 1857, to June 24, 1861, when graduated and appointed.

Second lieutenant, Second Cavalry, June 24, 1861; Fifth Cavalry, August 3, 1861; first lieutenant July 17, 1862.

Captain and additional aide de camp June 5, 1862, to March 31, 1863.

Brigadier general of volunteers June 29, 1863.

Major general of volunteers April 15, 1865.

Captain, Fifth Cavalry, May 8, 1864.

Lieutenant colonel, Seventh Cavalry, July 28, 1866.

He received the brevets of major July 3, 1863, "for gallant and meritorious services in the battle of Gettysburg, Pennsylvania"; of lieutenant colonel May 11, 1864, "for gallant and meritorious services in the battle of Yellow Tavern, Virginia"; of colonel September 19, 1864, "for gallant and meritorious services in the Battle of Winchester, Virginia"; of brigadier general March 13, 1865, "for gallant and meritorious services during the battle of Five Forks, Virginia"; of major general March 13, 1865, "for gallant and meritorious services during the campaign, ending in the surrender of the insurgent army of Northern Virginia"; and major general United States volunteers, "for gallant and meritorious services at the battles of Winchester and Fisher's Hill, Virginia," October 19, 1864.

He joined his regiment July 21, 1861, and served with it in the field, Virginia (participating in the battle of Bull Run, Virginia, July 21, 1861), to August 1, 1861, and in the defenses of Washington, D.C., to October 3, 1861; on sick leave to December 2, 1861; and with his regiment in the defenses of Washington, D.C., to March 10, 1862, and in the Army of the Potomac, in the Virginia Peninsular campaign, to April 22, 1862; assistant engineer of General W.F. Smith's division, Army of the Potomac, to May 28, 1862; aide-de-camp to General McClellan to March 31, 1863; with his regiment in the Army of the Potomac to June 6, 1863; aide-de-camp to General Pleasonton, commanding the cavalry corps, Army of the Potomac, to June 29, 1863; in command of the Second Brigade, Third Division, Cavalry Corps, Army of the Potomac to April 1864; the First Brigade, First Division, of that corps to September 30, 1864, and of the third cavalry division in the Middle Military Division to March 1865, and in the cavalry operations before Richmond to May 29, 1865; in command of the cavalry division of the Military Division of the Southwest from June 3 to July 17, 1865; of the cavalry forces of the Department of Texas to August 1865, and of the second cavalry division, Military Division of the Gulf, to November 13, 1865; chief of cavalry of the Department of Texas to February 1, 1866; on leave of absence to September 24, 1866; with regiment at Fort Riley, Kansas, to March 1867, and in the field in Kansas and Colorado to July 28, 1867; in command of his regiment in Kansas and the Indian territory to November 10, 1869; on leave to January 9, 1870; with his regiment in Kansas to January 11, 1871; on leave of absence to September 3, 1871; member of a board to inspect cavalry horses and on detached service at headquarters, Department of the South to May 22, 1872; with his regiment in command of the post of Elizabethtown, Kentucky, to February 1873; and at Memphis, Tennessee, to April 1873; in command of a battalion of his regiment enroute to and on the Yellowstone Expedition to September 1873; in command of Fort Abraham Lincoln, Dakota, to June 20, 1874; in command of the Black Hills Expedition to August 30, 1874, and of Fort Abraham Lincoln, Dakota, to October 2, 1874; on detached service at Chicago, Illinois, to November 15, 1875; in command of his regiment and Fort Abraham Lincoln, Dakota, to September 24, 1875; on leave of absence to February 15, 1876; on temporary duty at St. Paul, Minnesota, to March 12, 1876; commanding regiment at Fort Abraham Lincoln, Dakota, to March 20, 1876; witness before a committee of the House of Representatives to May 11, 1876; commanding his regiment at Fort Abraham Lincoln, Dakota, to May 16, 1876; in command of his regiment on an expedition against hostile Sioux Indians until he was killed in the battle of Little Big Horn River, Montana, June 25, 1876, and his whole command massacred.

J. C. Kelton
Adjutant-General

"Custer's career has few parallels in the history of any war in any country. His success was no more the result of luck than are the rewards of any human effort, for if there is any calling in life where the fruits are gathered in accordance with real merit it is in the profession of arms, where patient study, sleepless vigilance, laborious toil and iron nerve are requisite in order to reap the harvest of glory. Custer's luck was the result of judgement to do the right thing at the right time, and to his devotion to his profession and to his great energy and persistency."

Colonel Charles Francis Bates
United States Army

"Brave, but not reckless; self-confident, yet modest; ambitious, but regulating his conduct at all times by a high sense of honor and duty; eager for laurels, but scorning to wear them unworthily; ready and willing to act, but regardful of human life; quick in emergencies, cool and self-possessed, his courage was of the highest moral type, his perceptions were intuitions."

Personal Recollections of a
Cavalryman, by J.H. Kidd

"Verbal representations... may or may not have the merit of accuracy; yet photographic presentments of them will be accepted by posterity with an undoubting faith."—Alexander Gardner, 1865.

Portrait of Alexander Gardner, from the original carte de visite, courtesy of William A. Frassanito.

K-1—Seventeen-year-old George Armstrong Custer, June 1857, by H. Davis, Cadiz, Ohio. Copied from the unique, original 1/6-plate ambrotype, courtesy of Mary Ford and the Harrison County Historical Society.

1861

K-2—Cadet George Armstrong Custer, spring 1861, attributed to George Rockwood. Copied from the original, direct contact albumen print, from a June 1861 West Point Graduating Class Album, courtesy of West Point Museum.

K-3—Cadet Lieutenant George Armstrong Custer, on or about July 18, 1861, by an unknown New York photographer. Copied from the unique, original 1/4-plate ambrotype, courtesy of the National Portrait Gallery, Smithsonian Insitution.

1862

K-4—2nd Lieutenant George A. Custer, 5th U.S. Cavalry; 1st Lieutenant Nicholas Bowen, U. S. Engineers; 1st Lieutenant William Graham Jones, 10th U. S. Infantry, May 20, 1862, by James F. Gibson. From an original half stereo albumen print now in the collection of Henry Orgel.

K-5—Officers of General Andrew Porter's staff, May 20, 1862, by James F. Gibson. Standing from left: Captain Joseph Hancock Taylor, 6th U. S. Cavalry; Captain James McMillan, 2nd U. S. Infantry; Captain William Thomas Gentry, 17th U. S. Infantry; seated: 1st Lieutenant James William Forsyth, 18th U. S. Infantry; 2nd Lieutenant James (Scot) Stewart, 4th U. S. Artillery; 1st Lieutenant Charles F. Trowbridge, 15th Infantry; 1st Lieutenant William Graham Jones, 10th U. S. Infantry; reclining: 1st Lieutenant Nicholas Bowen, U. S. Engineers; 2nd Lieutenant George A. Custer, 5th U. S. Cavalry. From an original carte de visite, courtesy of Stephanie Lower. Negative number 389, published by Alexander Gardner as a stereoview and album gallery card.

"A camp photographer, seeing the two seated on a log, chatting, was preparing to photograph them, when young Washington called out to a small darkey standing near, and placed the child between them, saying the picture ought to be called 'Both sides, the cause.' And so it appeared in Harper's Weekly."

K-6 (top) and K-6V (bottom)— Lieutenant James Barroll Washington (Confederate prisoner, Custer's friend and classmate), a member of General Joseph E. Johnston's staff, captured at the Battle of Fair Oaks, Virginia, May 31, 1862, seated by 2nd Lieutenant George A. Custer, May 31, 1862, by James F. Gibson. From an original album gallery card in the author's collection; original stereoview courtesy of Custer Battlefield National Monument. Negative number 428, published by Alexander Gardner as a carte de visite.

K-7—Lieutenant James Barroll Washington and 2nd Lieutenant George A. Custer, May 31, 1862, by James F. Gibson. From an original contact print, from the original stereoview negative in the Library of Congress. Also published by Alexander Gardner as an album gallery card and carte de visite.

GARDNER, Photographer.

M. B. BRADY, Publisher.

THE PRESIDENT, GENERAL McCLELLAN AND SUITE
On the Battle-field of Antietam.

October 3, 1862.

K-9—Captain George Armstrong Custer, November 1862, by Edward P. Hipple, Philadelphia, Pennsylvania. From the unique, original, unpublished carte de visite, now in the collection of Jack M. Sterling.

K-8—*(opposite)* President Lincoln on the Battlefield of Antietam, October 3, 1862, by Alexander Gardner. From the earliest known original, direct-contact albumen print, from the lost original collodian negative, now in the collection of Joe Buberger. This was also published as plate 23, Gardner's Photographic Sketchbook of the Civil War, from a direct-contact copy negative in 1865-1866. Identified from left are: Colonel Delos B. Sacket, Captain George Monteith, Lieutenant Colonel Nelson B. Sweitzer, General George W. Morell, Colonel Alexander S. Webb, General George B. McClellan, Scout Adams, Dr. Jonathan Letterman, unidentified officer (sometimes identified as Custer), President Abraham Lincoln, Colonel Henry J. Hunt, General Fitz-John Porter, unidentified officer, Colonel Frederick T. Locke, General Andrew A. Humphreys, and Captain George Armstrong Custer.

There is much controversy regarding this image. The officer identified as Custer has been mis-identified as Colonel George A. Batchelder. Upon inspecting his portrait, this identification is determined to be incorrect. In 1946, author Roy Meredith illustrates a poor copy from the Library of Congress with printed captions, noting the unidentified officer to the right of Lincoln as Captain Custer. This identification is also incorrect. Examining the picture upon enlargement, and comparing it to the portrait taken by Hipple less than a month later, upholds my supposition. Gardner's own description found in his 1863 catalog states: "President Lincoln, Generals McClellan, Porter, Morell, Hunt, Humphrey, Colonel Sackett, Lieutenant Colonels Swietzer, Webb, Locke, Dr. Letterman, *Captain Custer*, and c., at Headquarters Fitz-John Porter, Antietam, October 1862." There are even those who claim that Custer is not in the picture, yet this too has been disproved.

1863

K-10 — Captain George Armstrong Custer, April 1863, by William H. Bowlsby, Monroe, Michigan. From the unique, original, unpublished carte de visite, in the author's collection.

K-11 — Captain George Armstrong Custer, April 1863, by William H. Bowlsby, Monroe, Michigan. Copied from the unique, original carte de visite, courtesy of the Monroe County Historical Commission.

K-12 — Captain George Armstrong Custer, April 1863, by William H. Bowlsby, Monroe, Michigan. From an original carte de visite, courtesy of Dr. Lawrence A. Frost.

K-13—*(Opposite)* Captain Leroy S. (Deacon) Elbert and Captain George A. Custer, end of April 1863, attributed to Henry Ulke, Washington, D.C. From the unique, unpublished, copy photograph of the lost original carte de visite in the collection of George Nas.

10

K-14—Captain George A. Custer and General Alfred Pleasonton, at General Pleasonton's headquarters, Falmouth, Virginia, first week of June 1863, by Timothy H. O'Sullivan. From an original contact print, from the original, direct-contact collodian negative in the Library of Congress.

K-14V—Captain George A. Custer at General Pleasonton's headquarters, Falmouth, Virginia, first week of June 1863, by Timothy H. O'Sullivan. From an original cabinet card, published by Levin C. Handy (Matthew Brady's nephew) in the author's collection.

K-15—Brigadier General George Armstrong Custer, on or about September 1863, and attributed to William Frank Browne. Copied from the unique, original, 1/2-plate ambrotype, courtesy of the National Portrait Gallery, Smithsonian Institution.

K-16—Brigadier General George Armstrong Custer, (not illustrated) 1/2-plate ambrotype taken at the same sitting. The image is highly oxidized, and shows slightly more of Custer's left hand and less of his right hand. Otherwise, the image is almost identical.

K-17—*(Opposite)* Brigadier General George Armstrong Custer, October 8, 1863, by Matthew Brady & Co., Washington, D.C. From the unique, original, contact print, from the original, unpublished, imperial collodian negative in the National Archives.

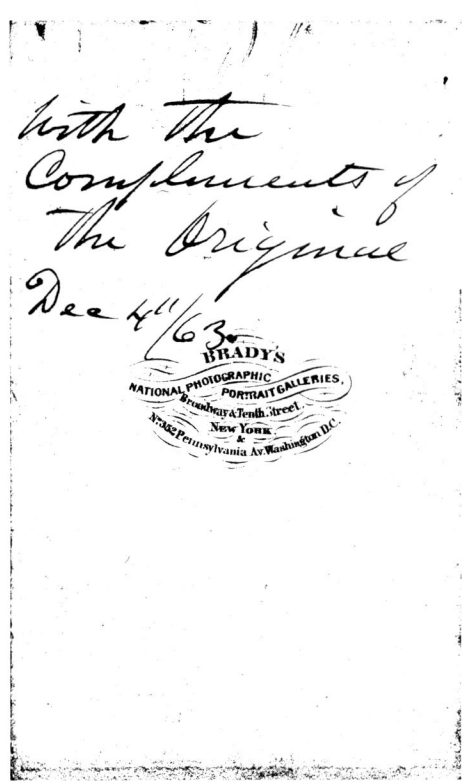

K-19—Brigadier General George Armstrong Custer, October 8, 1863, by Matthew Brady & Co. From the an original carte de visite, courtesy of Dale Anderson. Also shown is the verso of the image, personally inscribed by Custer.

K-18—*(Opposite)* Brigadier General George Armstrong Custer, October 8, 1863, by Matthew Brady & Co. From the unique, original, contact print, from the original, unpublished, imperial collodian negative in the National Archives.

K-20—Brigadier General George Armstrong Custer, October 8, 1863, by Matthew Brady & Co. Copied from an original, unpublished carte de visite now in the collection of Karl Rommel.

K-21—Brigadier General George Armstrong Custer, October 8, 1863, by Matthew Brady & Co. From an original, unpublished carte de visite, courtesy of Dale Anderson.

K-22—Brigadier General George Armstrong Custer, October 8, 1863, by Matthew Brady & Co. From an original carte de visite, courtesy of Dale Anderson.

K-23—Major General Alfred Pleasonton and personal aides and General George A. Custer. Taken at Warrenton, Virginia, October 9, 1863, by Timothy H. O'Sullivan. From an original, direct-contact albumen print in the author's collection. Standing, from left, are: 1st Lieutenant Benjamin Tucker Hutchins, 6th U.S. Cavalry; Lieutenant Von Koerner; Lieutenant James Franklin Wade, 6th U.S. Cavalry; 1st Lieutenant Gerrard Irvine Whitehead, 6th Pennsylvania Cavalry; 1st Lieutenant C. Thompson, 1st New York Cavalry; 1st Lieutenant George W. Yates, 4th Michigan Infantry; 1st Lieutenant D. W. Littlefield, 7th Michigan Cavalry. Seated, from left, are: 1st Lieutenant Leicester Walker, 5th U.S. Cavalry; 1st Lieutenant Henry Baker, 5th U.S. Cavalry; Major General Alfred Pleasonton; Brigadier General George A. Custer.

19

GEN. CUSTER AND GEN. PLEASONTON, WARRENTOWN, VA., OCTOBER, 1863.

K-24—General Custer and General Pleasonton at Warrenton, Virginia, October 9, 1863, by Timothy H. O'Sullivan. From an original, direct-contact albumen print, courtesy of David Hack.

K-24V—General George Armstrong Custer, at Warrenton, Virginia, October 9, 1863, by Timothy H. O'Sullivan. From an original, direct-contact albumen print, trimmed and mounted on an original carte de visite, published by Alexander Gardner, courtesy of Lloyd Ostendorf.

William Frank Browne

Custer's photographer, William Frank Browne. From the original tintype, and carte de visite (showing backmark) in the author's collection.

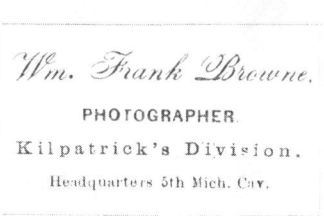
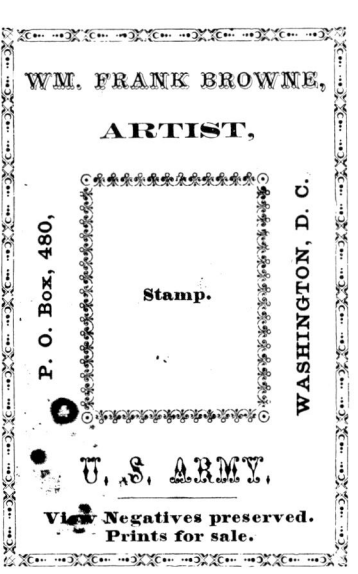

K-25—Brigadier General George Armstrong Custer in the uniform he would be married in, taken on or about January 25, 1864, by William Frank Browne. From an original, direct contact albumen print, courtesy of Karl Rommel. *(Opposite)*

1864

K-25—

K-26—

K-26V—

K-26 and K-26V (right)—Brigadier General George Armstrong Custer, on or about January 25, 1864, by William Frank Browne. From the unique, original, unpublished carte de visite now in the collection of Frank Mercantante. Also illustrated is a vignetted variant, having the distinction of being the only known carte having Browne's backmark. Image in the author's collection.

K-27—Brigadier General George Armstrong Custer, on or about January 25, 1864, by William Frank Browne. From the unique, original, unpublished carte de visite in the author's collection.

K-28—Brigadier General George Armstrong Custer, on or about February 15, 1864, by Matthew Brady & Co., New York. From the unique, original, unpublished carte de visite now in the collection of Darryl Lyons.

K-29—Brigadier General George Armstrong Custer, on or about February 15, 1864, by Matthew Brady & Co. From an original carte de visite now in the collection of Chester E. Nelson.

K-30—Brigadier General George Armstrong Custer, on or about February 15, 1864, by Matthew Brady & Co. From the unique original carte de visite courtesy of Lloyd Ostendorf.

K-31—Brigadier General George Armstrong Custer, on or about February 15, 1864, by Matthew Brady & Co. From the unique, original, unpublished carte de visite in the author's collection.

K-32—Brigadier General George A. Custer with his bride Elizabeth (Libbie) Custer, taken on or about February 15, 1864, by Matthew Brady & Co. From an original carte de visite courtesy of Dale Anderson.

K-33V—

K-33—Brigadier General George Armstrong Custer, on or about February 15, 1864, by Matthew Brady & Co. From an original contact print, from the original carte de visite collodian negative in the National Archives.
K-33V—(above right) An original carte de visite courtesy of Dale Anderson.

K-34—Brigadier General George A. Custer and his staff, at the headquarters of the Michigan Cavalry Brigade, Stevensburg, Virginia, February 1864, by an unknown photographer. From the unique, original, unpublished, glass lantern slide now in the collection of Custer Battlefield National Monument. Pictured are: Eliza, seated at the bottom of the stairs; Captain Jacob Greene, seated on steps; Brigadier General George A. Custer, seated on the chair; and Sergeant Michael Bellior, holding Custer's personal guidon.

K-36 and K-37—Brigadier General George Armstrong Custer, on or about May 1, 1864, by Matthew Brady & Co., Washington, D.C. From the unique, original contact print, from the original carte de viste collodian negative in the National Archives.

K-35—(opposite) Brigadier General George A. Custer and his staff, at the headquarters of the Michigan Cavalry Brigade, Stevensburg, Virginia, February 1864, by an unknown photographer. From the unique, original, imperial albumen print, courtesy of Custer Battlefield National Monument.

K-38—Brigadier General George Armstrong Custer at his headquarters in the field, Army of the Potomac, Virginia, on or about July 11, 1864, by Matthew Brady & Co. From the original stereoview in the author's collection.

This specific image till now has been misidentfied as Custer as a lieutenant. However, according to E. & H. T. Anthony's Catalog, this photograph was numbered 2438, which would fit into the camp portraits taken within this period, and was labeled "General."

K-39—Brigadier General George Armstrong Custer, on or about August 8, 1864, by M. J. Powers, employed by Jesse H. Whitehurst's Washington, D.C., Gallery. Copied from the unique, original, unpublished carte de visite, courtesy of the Harrison County Historical Society.

K-40—Brigadier General George A. Custer with Libbie, October 22, 1864, by Matthew Brady & Co., New York City. From the unique, original, unpublished carte de visite, courtesy of Dr. Lawrence A. Frost.

K-41—Brigadier General George A. Custer with Libbie, October 23, 1864, by Matthew Brady & Co., Washington, D.C. Copied from an original carte de visite, courtesy of the New York Public Library.

K-42—Brigadier General George A. Custer, Libbie Custer, and Miss Cora Bean, October 23, 1864, by Matthew Brady & Co. Copied from an original carte de visite, courtesy of the New York Public Library.

K-43—Brigadier General George Armstrong Custer, October 23, 1864, by Matthew Brady & Co. From an original carte de visite, courtesy of Dr. Lawrence A. Frost. The original contact print is from the original multiple-lens carte de viste collodian negative in the National Archives, **K-43V** (overleaf).

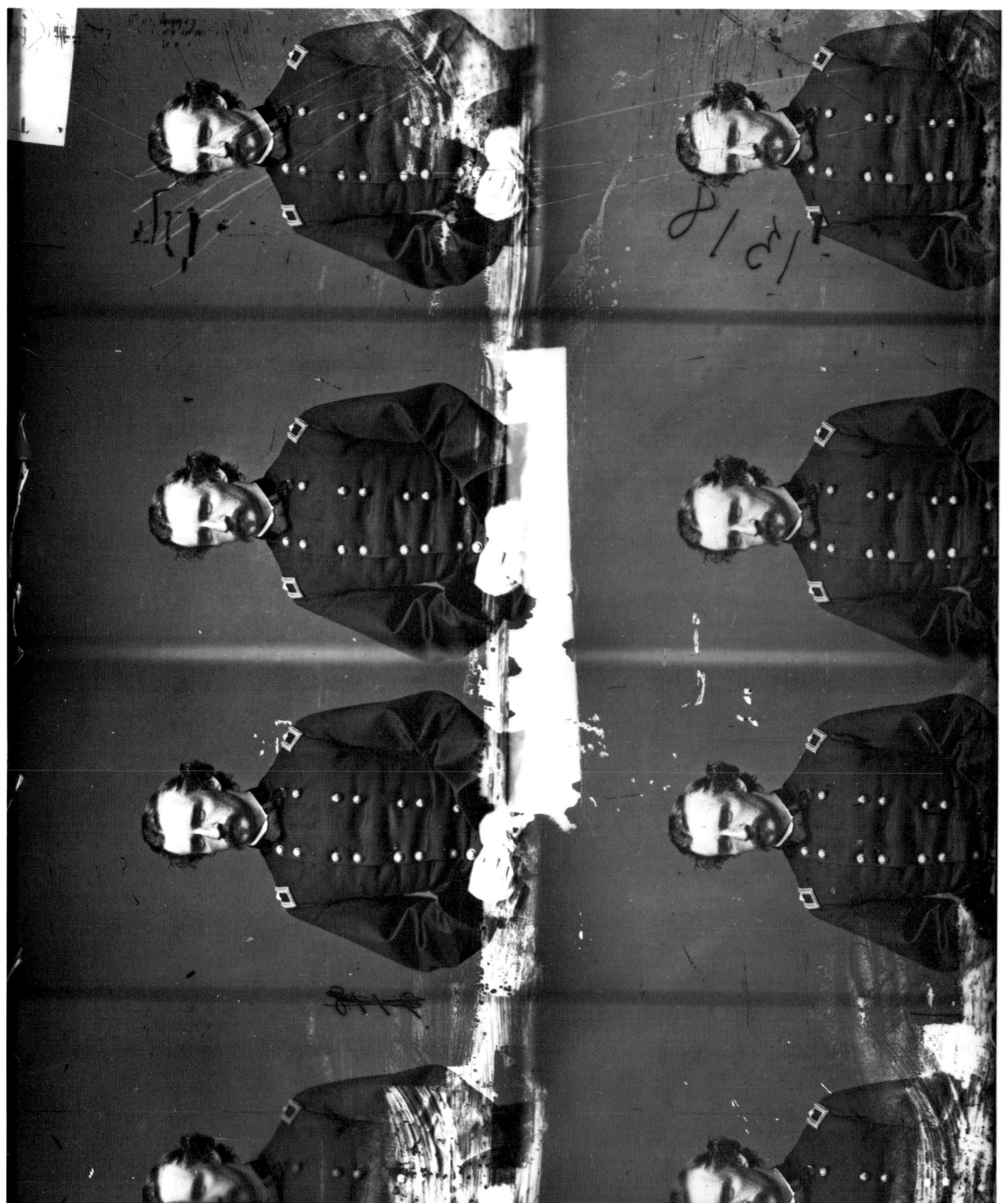

K-44—Brigadier General George Armstrong Custer, October 23, 1864, by Matthew Brady & Co. From an orginal contact print, from the original, direct contact, collodian negative in the Library of Congress.

K-45—Major General George A. Custer and staff at the M.Y. Mason mansion, Winchester, Virginia, December 25, 1864, by William H. Bowlsby, Monroe, Michigan. From an original, direct-contact albumen print, courtesy of Custer Battlefield National Monument. Identified, from left, are: Joseph Fought, orderly; Colonel Edward W. Whitaker; Lieutenant Thomas W. Custer, Surgeon L.P. Woods, Elizabeth B. Custer, Judge Daniel S. Bacon, Major General George A. Custer, Mrs. Rhonda Bacon, Miss Mary Richmond, Mrs. Woods, Henry Mail, Lieutenant Frederick A. Nimms, Colonel Jacob Greene, Baron Sieb, Captain Charles W. Lee, Lieutenant James Christiency, Lieutenant E. V. Norvell, and an unknown scout.

K-46—*(Overleaf)* General Philip Sheridan and his staff, January 2, 1865, by Alexander Gardner. From the unique, original, imperial platinum print, published in 1892 by Moses Preston Rice, in the author's collection. Identified, from left, are: Generals Wesley Merritt, Philip Sheridan, George Crook, James William Forsyth, and George A. Custer.

1865

K-47—Major General George Armstrong Custer, January 2, 1865, by Alexander Gardner. From the unique, original, unpublished carte de visite in the author's collection.

K-48—Major General George Armstrong Custer, January 2, 1865, by Alexander Gardner. From the unique, original, unpublished carte de visite now in the collection of Chester E. Nelson.

K-49—Major General George A. Custer, Lieutenant Thomas Ward Custer, Elizabeth B. Custer, January 3, 1865, by Matthew Brady & Co., Washington, D.C. From an original carte de visite in the author's collection.

K-50—Major General George Armstrong Custer, January 3, 1865, by Matthew Brady & Co. From an original, unpublished carte de visite, courtesy of Dr. Lawrence A. Frost.

K-51—Major General George Armstrong Custer, January 3, 1865, by Matthew Brady & Co. From an original, unpublished contact print, from the unpublished collodian carte de visite negative in the Library of Congress.

K-52—Major General George Armstrong Custer, January 3, 1865, by Matthew Brady & Co. From an original, direct-contact collodian negative from the Department of Photographic History, American History Museum, Smithsonian Institution.

K-53—General Philip H. Sheridan and his staff, January 3, 1865, by Matthew Brady & Co. From an original contact print, from the unpublished direct-contact collodian negative in the Library of Congress. Identified, from left, are: Generals Philip H. Sheridan, James Forsyth, Wesley Merritt, Thomas C. Devin, and George A. Custer.

K-54—*(Overleaf)* General Philip H. Sheridan and his staff, January 3, 1865, by Matthew Brady & Co. From an original contact print, from an original, imperial collodian negative in the National Archives. Identified, from left, are: Generals Philip H. Sheridan, James Forsyth, Wesley Merritt, Thomas C. Devin, and George A. Custer.

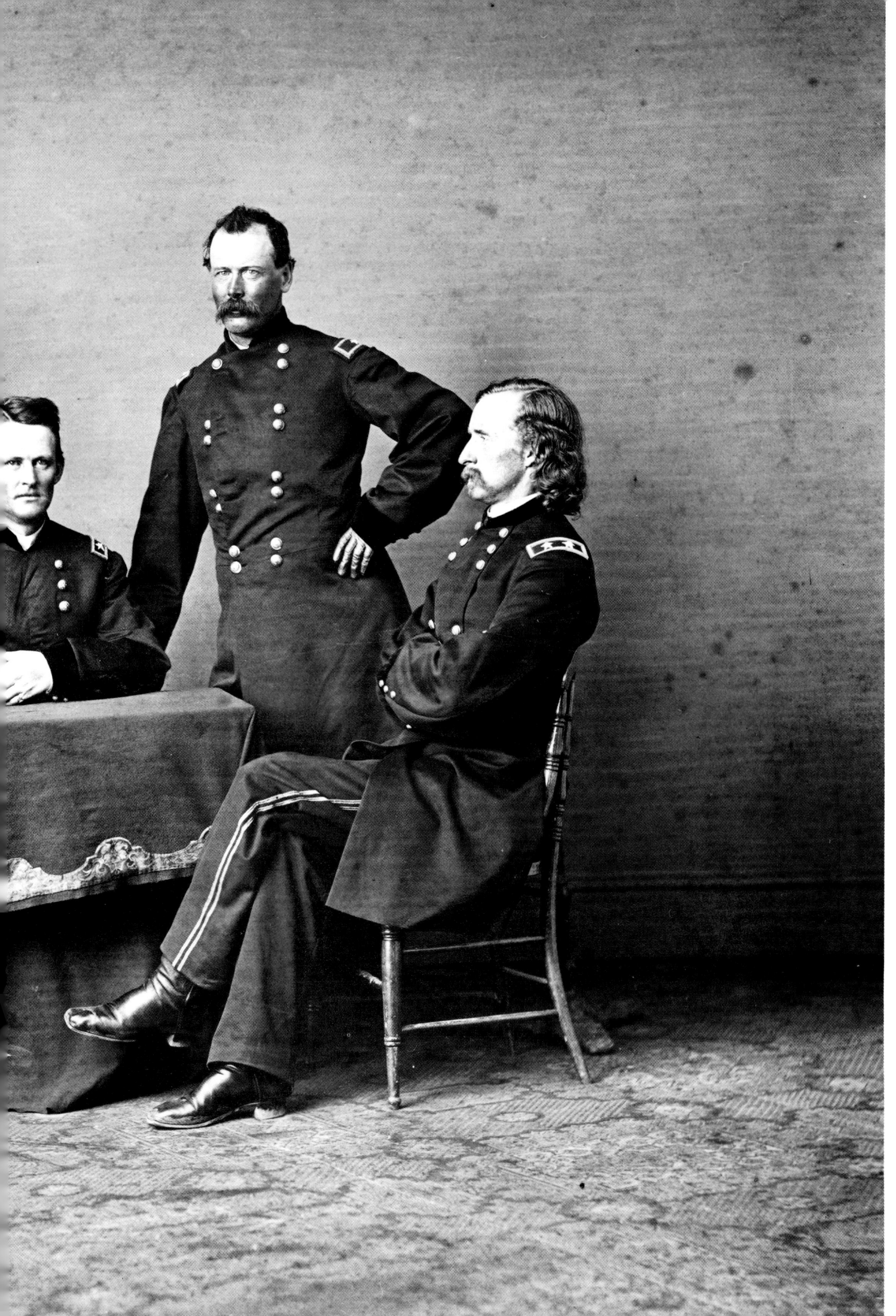

K-56 and K-56V—*(Right)* Major General George Armstrong Custer, January 3, 1865, by Matthew Brady & Co. From an original proof albumen print, courtesy of George R. Rinhart. **K-56V**—An original carte de visite in the author's collection.

K-55—*(Preceding)* General Philip H. Sheridan and his staff, January 3, 1865, by Matthew Brady & Co. From an original contact print, from an original, imperial albumen print, courtesy of the Custer Battlefield National Monument. Identified, from left, are: Generals Philip H. Sheridan, James Forsyth, Wesley Merritt, Thomas C. Devin, and George A. Custer.

K-57—

K-57V—

K-57 and K-57V—Major General George Armstrong Custer, January 4, 1865, by Matthew Brady & Co., New York. From an original, unpublished carte de visite in the author's collection. **K-57V**—Proof photograph, courtesy of Dale Anderson.

K-58—Major General George Armstrong Custer, January 4, 1865, by Matthew Brady & Co. From the unique, original carte de visite, courtesy of Craig Haffner.

K-59—Major General George Armstrong Custer, January 4, 1865, by Matthew Brady & Co. From an original carte de visite, courtesy of Craig Haffner. **K-59V**—*(Overleaf)* Image also published as a stereoview, using the multiple lens negative in the 1880s by Taylor & Huntington, courtesy of Dale Anderson.

K-59V—Major General George Armstrong Custer, January 4, 1865, by Matthew Brady & Co.

K-60—Major General George Armstrong Custer, January 4, 1865, by Matthew Brady & Co. From an original contact print, from the unique, original, collodian carte de visite negative in the National Archives.

K-61—Major General George Armstrong Custer, January 4, 1865, by Matthew Brady & Co. From an original contact print, from the original, unpublished, direct-contact collodian negative in the National Archives.

K-62—*(Opposite)* Major General George Armstrong Custer, January 4, 1865, by Matthew Brady & Co. From an original contact print, from the unique, original, unpublished, imperial collodian negative in the National Archives.

K-63—Major General George A. Custer and Libbie, on or about April 12, 1865, attributed to William Frank Browne. Copied from *Custer's Libbie* with the permission of Dr. Lawrence A. Frost. From the lost unique original 1/16th plate tintype, courtesy of Dr. Lawrence A. Frost.

K-64—Major General George A. Custer, Libbie, and Eliza, on or about April 12, 1865, attributed to William Frank Browne. From the unique original 1/16th plate tintype, courtesy of Custer Battlefield National Monument.

K-65—Major General George A. Custer, Libbie, and an unidentified member of his brigade, on or about April 12, 1865, and attributed to William Frank Browne. From the unique, original, unpublished 1/16th plate tintype courtesy of Michael and Regina Swygert-Smith in trust for the Custer Battlefield National Monument.

K-66—Major General George Armstrong Custer, May 1865, by John Goldin & Co., Washington, D.C. Copied from the unique, original, unpublished carte de visite in the Library of Congress.

K-67—Major General George Armstrong Custer, May 1865, by John Goldin & Co. Copied from the unique, original carte de visite, courtesy of the United States Army Military History Institute.

K-68 — Major General George Armstrong Custer, May 1865, by John Goldin & Co. From the unique, original, unpublished carte de visite in the author's collection.

K-69 — Major General George Armstrong Custer, May 1865, by John Goldin & Co. From the unique, contemporary copy of an unpublished carte de visite published by Peck Brothers, courtesy of Dale Anderson.

K-70—Major General George Armstrong Custer, May 1865, by John Goldin & Co. From an original, unpublished carte de visite, courtesy of Dale Anderson.

K-71—Major General George Armstrong Custer, May 1865, by John Goldin & Co. From an original, unpublished carte de visite now in the collection of John W. Painter.

K-72—*(Left)* Major General George Armstrong Custer, May 1865, by Matthew Brady & Co., Washington, D.C. From an original carte de visite, courtesy of Dale Anderson.

K-73 (left) and K-73V (above)—Major General George Armstrong Custer, May 1865, by Matthew Brady & Co. From an original carte de visite now in the collection of Craig Haffner. The proof carte de visite (K-73V) is courtesy of Dale Anderson.

K-74—Major General George Armstrong Custer, May 1865, by Matthew Brady & Co. From an original contact print from the original multiple-lens collodian carte de visite negative in the National Archives.

K-75—Major General George Armstrong Custer, May 1865, by Matthew Brady & Co. From an original contact print, from the unique, original direct-contact collodian negative in the National Archives.

K-76—(*Opposite*) Major General George Armstrong Custer, May 1865, by Matthew Brady & Co. From the unique, original contact print, from the original, direct-contact collodian negative in the Library of Congress.

K-76V—Major General George Armstrong Custer, May 1865, by Matthew Brady & Co. From an original cabinet card in the 1880s by Levin C. Handy (Brady's nephew) in the author's collection.

K-77—Major General George Armstrong Custer, May 23, 1865, by Matthew Brady & Co. From an original contact print, from the unique, original, direct-contact collodian negative in the Department of Photography, American History Museum, Smithsonian Institution.

Although this is one of the most famous and popular photographs of Custer, its history remains shrouded in mystery. As of this date, there are no contemporary albumen prints known to exist. Even though this was perhaps Custer's favorite likeness (his wall was adorned by an enlarged copy photograph), his wife's collection contained no original. In 1865, Matthew Brady issued a contemporary photographic engraving, K-77V, courtesy of Joe Gustin (overleaf), yet there is no record of the original plate. In the early 1950s, George L. Andrews discovered 44 well-wrapped collodian negatives in his carriage house on Front Street, Owego, New York. Apparently, the collection originated from Andrew Burgess, a past manager of Brady's gallery toward the end of Brady's life. Burgess most likely passed them on from relative to relative until they were willed to George Andrews' mother. In the 1960s, Andrews sold the collection to GAF Corporation, which donated them to the Smithsonian Institution in Washington, D.C.

Note written on the verso of a carte de visite in Custer's hand, dating the photograph, courtesy of Brigham Young University.

K-77V-A signed carte de visite now in a private collection.

K-78V—

K-78-Major General George Armstrong Custer, May 23, 1865 by Matthew Brady & Co,
From an original carte de visite courtesy of Arthur C. Unger. Also published as a contemporary
copy tintype (K-78V) courtesy of Custer Battlefield National Monument.

K-79—Major General George Armstrong Custer, May 23, 1865, by Matthew Brady & Co. From an original contact print, from the unique, original, direct-contact collodian negative in the Library of Congress.

A full description of Custer's uniform he wore on the day of the Grand Review, May 23, 1865, as photographed by Matthew Brady. From an original note in the hand of Elizabeth B. Custer, courtesy of Dale Anderson *(overle*

The photograph of Maj. Gen'l George A. Custer at time of his years of age, is a copy of one taken by Brady of Washington. He had photographed that full-[length?] of Gen'l Gen. General Custer is in undress uniform. The iron felt hat was captured from a Confederate officer. The shirt of blue flannel was purchased from the Government gun boat in the Potomac river. The necktie was scarlet. General Custer began to wear the cut as shown he was made a Brigadier General and assigned the command of the Michigan Cavalry Brigade. The entire Brigade adopted the tie and then the General was appointed Major General and given command of the 3rd Cavalry Division of the Army of the Potomac, they also wore them. The badge on the tie was that of the Michigan Brigade with the motto of the State and the name of Custer.

Elizabeth B. Custer

K-80—General Custer rides in the Grand Review on top of a fiery racehorse named Don Juan. Just prior to his arrival at the reviewing stand, the horse bolts, knocking Custer's hat from his head. Custer displayed excellent horsemanship while controlling the horse. Taken May 23, 1865, and attributed to E. & H. T. Anthony. From the unique, original, unpublished stereoview now in the collection of Henry Orgel.

K-81—Major General George Armstrong Custer, July 1865, while in New Orleans, Louisiana, by an unknown photographer. From the unique, original, unpublished 1/4-plate tintype courtesy of a private collector.

K-82—Mrs. Elizabeth B. Custer and Major General George A. Custer, October 18, 1865, at Hempstead, Texas, by an unknown photographer. Copied from the unique, original, 1/4-plate tintype, courtesy of West Point Library.

K-84—Major General George Armstrong Custer and Elizabeth B. Custer, October 18, 1865, at Hempstead, Texas, by an unknown photographer. Copied from the unique, original, unpublished multiple-lens carte de visite-sized tintype, courtesy of Dr. Roland Bill.

K-83—*(Overleaf)* Mrs. Carrie Farnham Lyon and Major General George A. Custer, October 18, 1865, at Hempstead, Texas, by an unknown photographer. From an imperial gelatin silver copy photograph, from the lost original, 1/4-plate tintype, courtesy of Custer Battlefield National Monument.

K-85—Custer's headquarters, Blind Asylum, Austin, Texas, November 1865, by a unknown photographer. From the unique, original, direct-contact albumen print, courtesy of Custer Battlefield National Monument.

K-86—Custer's headquarters, Blind Asylum, Austin, Texas, November 1865, by a unknown photographer. From the unique, original, direct-contact albumen print, courtesy of Custer Battlefield National Monument. Identified, from left, are: Charles Kendall, two unidentified men, Rebecca Richmond, Mary Richmond, Colonel Thomas W. Custer, Major General George A. Custer, Mrs. Elizabeth B. Custer, Eliza, father Emanuel Custer, Colonel Jacob Greene, and an unidentified person. *(Overleaf)*

1866-1868

K-87—Major General George A. Custer and Libbie, on or about September 1866, during President Andrew Johnson's "swing around the circle," by an unknown photographer. From the unique, original, carte de visite in the author's collection.

K-88—Mrs. Rose Flint, George A. Custer, Libbie, and an unidentified couple, at Dundee, Michigan, March 1868, by an unknown photographer. Copied from a modern copy photograph, from the unique carte de visite, courtesy of Dr. Lawrence A. Frost.

K-89—Rebecca Richmond; Charles Kendall; Mrs. Mary Richmond Kendall; Lt. Colonel George A. Custer; Libbie Custer, on or about January 1868 by Jay Noble & Co., Leavenworth, Kansas. From the unique, original, unpublished carte de visite courtesy of Michael and Regina Swygert-Smith in trust for the Custer Battlefield National Monument.

K-90—Rebecca Richmond, Mrs. Mary Richmond Kendall, Charles Kendall, Lieutenant Colonel George A. Custer, Libbie Custer, on or about January 1868, by Jay Noble & Co., Leavenworth, Kansas. From the unique, original, direct-contact albumen print, courtesy of Custer Battlefield National Monument.

K-91—Camp "Sandy" Forsyth, 7th U.S. Cavalry on the Arkansas River, October 1868, prior to the Washita Campaign, by an unknown photographer. Copied from the unique, original, direct-contact albumen print, courtesy of the Beinecke Rare Book and Manuscript Library, Yale University. Identified, from the left, are: Assistant Surgeon Henry Lippincott, Captain William Thompson, Company B; Charley Thompson, 1st Lieutenant Matthew Berry, Company C; 2nd Lieutenant Thomas J. March, Company G; 2nd Lieutenant H. Walworth Smith, Company D; 1st Lieutenant David W. Wallingford, Company B (seated); Captain Albert Barnitz, Company G (seated); Captain Lee P. Gillette, Company C; Captain Edward Myers, Company E (middle); 1st Lieutenant Charles Brewster, Company I; 1st Lieutenant Samuel M. Robbins, Company D; Captain George W. Yates, Company F; Major Joel H. Elliott (seated); Assistant Surgeon Charles S. DeGraw; 1st Lieutenant Myles Moylan, adjutant, 7th U.S. Cavalry (seated); Captain Louis M. Hamilton, Company A (middle); Captain Thomas B. Weir, Company D; Lieutenant Colonel George A. Custer (seated); 1st Lieutenant William W. Cooke, Company H, 1st Lieutenant T. S. Wallace, 3rd U.S. Infantry (middle); 1st Lieutenant Owen Hale, Company M; 2nd Lieutenant Edward Law, Company K; 1st Lieutenant Thomas W. Custer (seated); 2nd Lieutenant Francis M. Gibson, Company F; Assistant Surgeon William C. Rennick (on knee); 1st Lieutenant Edward F. Godfrey, Company K; 2nd Lieutenant Edward G. Mathey, Company I (seated); and 1st Lieutenant James M. Bell (seated).

K-92—Camp "Sandy" Forsyth, on the Arkansas River, October 1868, prior to the Washita Campaign, by an unknown photographer. Copied from the unique, original, unpublished, direct-contact albumen print, courtesy of the Beinecke Rare Book and Manuscript Library, Yale University. Identified, from the left, are: Captain William Thompson, 1st Lieutenant Matthew Berry, Charley Thompson, Captain George W. Yates, 1st Lieutenant David W. Wallingford (seated), 2nd Lieutenant Walworth Smith, Captain Albert Barnitz (seated), Captain Lee P. Gillette (beyond Myers), Captain Edward Myers, Major Joel H. Elliott (seated), Assistant Surgeon Henry Lippincott (middle), 1st Lieutenant Samuel M. Robbins, Captain Thomas B. Weir, 1st Lieutenant Myles Moylan (seated), 1st Lieutenant William W. Cooke, 1st Lieutenant T. S. Wallace (middle), 1st Lieutenant Owen Hale, Lieutenant Colonel George A. Custer (seated profile), 2nd Lieutenant Edward Law, 1st Lieutenant Thomas W. Custer (seated profile), 2nd Lieutenant Francis M. Gibson, 2nd Lieutenant Thomas J. March (behind Gibson), 1st Lieutenant Edward F. Godfrey, Assistant Surgeon William C. Rennick (on knee), Assistant Surgeon Charles S. Degraw, Captain Louis M. Hamilton, 2nd Lieutenant Edward G. Mathey (seated), 1st Lieutenant Charles Brewster, and 1st Lieutenant James M. Bell.

K-93—Lieutenant Colonel George Armstrong Custer, holding his Spencer carbine, Fort Dodge, Kansas, November 1868, by an unknown photographer. From the unique, original, direct-contact albumen print, courtesy of Custer Battlefield National Monument.

K-94—*(Overleaf)* Lieutenant Colonel George Armstrong Custer, with his Osage Indian scouts, Fort Dodge, Kansas, November 1868, by an unknown photographer. From the unique, original, direct-contact albumen print, courtesy of Custer Battlefield National Monument.

1 tent
2 Girls that called is nae, hopie
    eshe John —
    boy scouts
3 Police support is new, Americanment
    he was the Penn

boy of leg

K-95—Lieutenant Colonel George Armstrong Custer, February 9, 1868, at Fort Sill, Wichita Mountains, 35 miles from Fort Cobb, Indian Territory, by an unknown photographer. From the unique, contemporary albumen print, copied from the lost original tintype, courtesy of Custer Battlefield National Monument.

1869

K-96—Lieutenant Colonel George A. Custer, Libbie Custer, and Lieutenant Thomas W. Custer on the porch rail behind their tent. Camp on the Big Creek, near Fort Hays, Kansas, summer 1869, attributed to W. J. Phillips, Preston, Missouri. From the unique, original, direct-contact albumen print, courtesy of Custer Battlefield National Monument.

K-97—Camp on the Big Creek, near Fort Hays, Kansas, summer 1869, attributed to W. J. Phillips, Preston, Missouri. From an original, direct-contact albumen print, courtesy of Custer Battlefield National Monument. Identified, from left, are: Unidentified 7th Cavalry trooper, Lieutenant Colonel George A. Custer, Dr. Dunbar, Mrs. Elizabeth B. Custer, and Lieutenant Thomas W. Custer, Mrs. A. E. Smith, and Mrs. Donald McIntosh.

K-98—*(Overleaf)* Camp on the Big Creek, near Fort Hays, Kansas, summer 1869, attributed to W. J. Phillips, Preston, Missouri. From an original, direct-contact albumen print, courtesy of Custer Battlefield National Monument. Identified, from left, are: Lieutenant Thomas W. Custer, Mrs. Elizabeth B. Custer, Lieutenant Colonel George A. Custer, Dr. Dunbar, Mrs. A. E. Smith, and Mrs. Donald McIntosh.

K-99—Mealtime on the Big Creek, near Fort Hays, Kansas, summer 1869, attributed to W. J. Phillips, Preston, Missouri. From an original, direct-contact albumen print, courtesy of Custer Battlefield National Monument. Identified, from left, are: Lieutenant Colonel George A. Custer, Elizabeth B. Custer, and an unidentified orderly.

K-100—*(Overleaf)* Camp on the Big Creek, near Fort Hays, Kansas, summer 1869, attributed to W. J. Phillips, Preston, Missouri. From an original, direct-contact albumen print, courtesy of Custer Battlefield National Monument. Identified, from left, are: Dr. Dunbar; Mrs. Elizabeth B. Custer; Mr. J. R. Young, *New York Tribune*; Captain Thomas B. Weir; Mrs. Nettie Smith; Lieutenant Colonel George A. Custer; Mr. Lamborn, secretary of the Union Pacific Railroad; Mrs. Donald McIntosh; 2nd Lieutenant Francis M. Gibson.

K-101—Buffalo hunt, near Big Creek, Kansas, September 1869, by W. J. Phillips, Preston, Missouri. From the unique, original, cabinet card, courtesy of Custer Battlefield National Monument. Identified, from left, are: An orderly, Lieutenant Henry J. Nowlan, sutler Hill P. Wilson, Captain Thomas Weir, 1st Lieutenant James M. Bell, 2nd Lieutenant Francis M. Gibson, Lieutenant Colonel George A. Custer, Captain Frederick Benteen, 1st Lieutenant Thomas W. Custer, Captain William Thompson, and Charley Thompson.

K-102—*(Overleaf)* Buffalo hunt, near Big Creek, Kansas, September 1869, by W. J. Phillips, Preston, Missouri. From the original, direct-contact albumen print, courtesy of Custer Battlefield National Monument. Identified, from left, are: Lieutenant Colonel George A. Custer, Miss Talmadge, Captain William Thompson, Lord Waterpark, Lord Paget, Lieutenant Myles Moylan, Captain Thomas Weir, Colonel Samuel D. Sturgis, Lieutenant William W. Cooke, Mrs. Elizabeth B. Custer, Lieutenant Thomas W. Custer, Captain Brewster, Mrs. Godfrey, Mr. Talmadge.

K-103—Buffalo hunt, near Big Creek, Kansas, September 1869, by W. J. Phillips, Preston, Missouri. Copied from the original, direct-contact albumen print, courtesy of West Point Special Collections. Identified, from left, are: Lieutenant Colonel George A. Custer, Miss Talmadge, Frank Talmadge, Captain William Thompson, Lord Waterpark, Lord Paget, Lieutenant Myles Moylan, Captain Thomas B. Weir, Lieutenant James M. Bell, Colonel Samuel D. Sturgis, Lieutenant William W. Cooke, Lieutenant Henry J. Noylan, Mrs. Elizabeth B. Custer, Lieutenant Thomas W. Custer, Mr. Smith, Mrs. Godfrey, Captain Brewster, Mr. Talmadge.

K-104—Lieutenant Colonel George Armstrong Custer, December 1869, by Matthew Brady & Co., Washington, D.C. From an original cabinet card, courtesy of Custer Battlefield National Monument.

K-105—Lieutenant Colonel George Armstrong Custer, December 1869, by Matthew Brady & Co. From an original contact print, from the unique, original, unpublished, cabinet card collodian negative in the Library of Congress.

1871

K-106— Lieutenant Colonel George A. Custer and veterans of the War of 1812, July 4, 1871, by Simon Wing, Monroe, Michigan. Copied from the unique, original, direct-contact albumen print, courtesy of the Monroe County Historical Commission. Taken at the residence of Joseph Guyor, Guyor's Island, two miles east of Monroe, Michigan. Top row, left: John Beshear; John Clapper, age 76; Lieutenant Colonel George A. Custer; Francis Lazarre, age 82; Jean DeChovin, age 77. Center row, left: John B. Beaseau, age 80; George Younglove, age 77; Fred Boroff, age 100 years, 7 months; David Van Pelt, age 89; Louis Jacobs, age 96; Charles Hixon, age 76; Henry Mason, age 79; Thomas Whelpley, age 73; Joseph Guyor, age 88. Bottom row, left: Peter Navarre, age 82; James B. Nadeau, age 77; Emmanuel Custer; Robert F. Navarre, age 80; Joseph Foulke, age 80; Bronson French, age 82.

1872

K-107—Lieutenant Colonel George Armstrong Custer, on or about January 1872 and attributed to E. L. Eaton, Omaha, Nebraska. Copied from the unique, original, unpublished direct-contact albumen print, courtesy Kansas State Historical Society.

K-108—Hunting party with the Grand Duke, Alexis, on or about January 22, 1872, by J. Lee Knight, Topeka, Kansas. From the original, imperial albumen print, courtesy of Custer Battlefield National Monument. Standing, from left, are: Frank Thompson, Dr. Condrin, Colonel George Alexander Forsyth, Count Olsonfieff, Major M. V. Asche, Colonel Nelson Bowman Sweitzer, and Lieutenant Tudor. Seated, from left, are: Consul Bodisco;

Chancellor Machin; Lieutenant General Philip H. Sheridan; the Grand Duke, Alexis; Admiral Possiet; and Lieutenant Colonel George A. Custer. Seated on floor, from left, are: Lieutenant Colonel James William Forsyth, Lieutenant Sterlegoff, and Lieutenant Colonel Michael Vincent Sheridan.

PHOTOGRAPH BY J. LEE KNIGHT, TOPEKA, KANSAS. Entered according to Act of Congress, in the year 1872, by J. Lee Knight, in the Office of the Librarian of Congress, at Washington, D. C. STATE RECORD PRINTING HOUSE, TOPEKA, KANSAS.

Gen. Geo. A. Custer.   Col. G. A. Forsyth.   LIEUT. GEN. P. H. SHERIDAN.   Maj. M. V. Asche.   Col. M. V. Sheridan.   Gen. N. B. Sweitzer.   Gen. J. W. Forsyth.

K-110—

K-110 and K-110V—Lieutenant Colonel George Armstrong Custer, on or about January 24, 1872, by James A. Scholten. From an original cabinet card now in the collection of Andrew Monte. **K-110V**—The autographed cabinet card, courtesy of Dr. Lawrence A. Frost.

K-109—*(Opposite)* Lieutenant General Philip H. Sheridan and staff, on or about January 22, 1872, by J. Lee Knight, Topeka, Kansas. From an original, imperial albumen print, courtesy of Custer Battlefield National Monument. Standing, from left, are: Lieutenant Colonel George Alexander Forsyth, Major M. V. Asche, and Lieutenant Colonel Michael Vincent Sheridan. Seated, from left, are: Lieutenant Colonel George A. Custer, Lieutenant General Philip H. Sheridan, Lieutenant Colonel Nelson Bowman Sweitzer, Lieutenant Colonel James William Forsyth.

K-110V—

K-111—Lieutenant Colonel George Armstrong Custer, on or about January 24, 1872, by James A. Scholten. From the unique, original cabinet card, courtesy of Custer Battlefield National Monument.

K-112—Lieutenant Colonel George Armstrong Custer, on or about January 24, 1872, by James A. Scholten. From the unique, original, unpublished cabinet card, courtesy of Custer Battlefield National Monument.

K-113—Lieutenant Colonel George Armstrong Custer, on or about January 24, 1872, by James A. Scholten. From an original cabinet-sized insert, published in "Photographic World," courtesy of Andrew Monte.

K-114—Lieutenant Colonel George A. Custer and the Grand Duke, Alexis, on or about January 24, 1872, by James A. Scholten. Copied from the unique, original, unpublished cabinet card in the Library of Congress.

K-115—*(Opposite)* Lieutenant Colonel George A. Custer and the Grand Duke, Alexis, on or about January 24, 1872, by James A. Scholten. From the unique, original, imperial albumen print, courtesy of Custer Battlefield National Monument.

K-116—Lieutenant Colonel George A. Custer, March 1873, by Bingham and Craver, Memphis, Tennessee. From the unique, original, imperial albumen print, courtesy of Custer Battlefield National Monument.

1873

K-117—Lieutenant Colonel George A. Custer, March 1873, by Bingham and Craver, Memphis, Tennessee. From the unique, original, direct-contact albumen print, courtesy of Custer Battlefield National Monument.

K-117V—

K-117V—Lieutenant Colonel George A. Custer, March 1873. A contemporary copy carte de visite issued by Simon Wing, Monroe, Michigan, copied from the original albumen print by Bingham and Craver for all patrons having their portraits taken. Carte de visite now in the collection of Frank Mercantante; newspaper advertisement courtesy of Monroe County Historical Commission.

K-118—Lieutenant Colonel George Armstrong Custer with the "King of the Forest," killed during the Yellowstone Expedition, September 6, 1873, by William R. Pywell. From the unique, original, unpublished stereoview, courtesy of Wilfred Thompson.

K-118V—An original, contemporary, autographed copy albumen print courtesy of Custer Battlefield National Monument.

K-119—Custer's quarters, Fort Abraham Lincoln, by Orlando S. Goff. From the unique, original, direct-contact albumen print, courtesy of Custer Battlefield National Monument. Identified, from left, are: Lieutenant Colonel George A. Custer, Mrs. Margaret C. Calhoun, Lieutenant James Calhoun, Mrs. Annie Yates, Miss Agnes Bates, Mrs. Elizabeth B. Custer, and Captain William Thompson.

K-120—On the steps at Custer's quarters, Fort Abraham Lincoln, November 1873, by Orlando S. Goff. From the unique, original, direct-contact albumen print, courtesy of Custer Battlefield National Monument. Identified, from left, top row, are: Miss Agnes Bates, Lieutenant James Calhoun, and Mrs. Margaret Custer Calhoun. Center row: Mrs. Elizabeth B. Custer, Lieutenant Colonel George A. Custer, Fred Calhoun (front of Custer) and Captain William Thompson.

K-121—At Custer's quarters, Fort Abraham Lincoln, November 1873, by Orlando S. Goff. From the unique, original, direct-contact albumen print, courtesy of Custer Battlefield National Monument. Identified, from left, are: 2nd Lieutenant Nelson Bronson, 6th U.S. Infantry; 2nd Lieutenant George D. Wallace; Lieutenant Colonel George A. Custer; Mrs. Thomas McDougall; Captain John S. Poland, 6th U.S. Infantry; Mrs. Elizabeth B. Custer; 2nd Lieutenant Benjamin Hodgson; Assistant Surgeon J. V. T. Middleton; Miss Agnes Bates; 2nd Lieutenant Charles Varnum; Charles Thompson; 1st Lieutenant Thomas M. McDougall; Captain George Yates; Mrs. Margaret Custer Calhoun; Mrs. Yates; Lieutenant Colonel William P. Carlin, 17th U.S. Infantry; Captain William Thompson; 1st Lieutenant Thomas W. Custer; Mrs. Myles Moylan; Mrs. McIntosh; 1st Lieutenant Myles Moylan; 2nd Lieutenant Donald McIntosh.

K-122—At Custer's quarters, Fort Abraham Lincoln, November 1873, by Orlando S. Goff. From an original, direct-contact albumen print, courtesy of Dale Anderson. Identified, from left, are: 2nd Lieutenant Nelson Bronson, 2nd Lieutenant George D. Wallace; Lieutenant Colonel George A. Custer, 2nd Lieutenant Benjamin Hodgson, Mrs. Elizabeth B. Custer, Mrs. Thomas McDougall, 1st Lieutenant Thomas M. McDougall, Dr. J. V. T. Middleton, Mrs. Annie Yates, Captain George W. Yates; Charles W. Thompson, Mrs. Margaret Custer Calhoun, Miss Agnes Bates, Captain John S. Poland, 2nd Lieutenant Charles Varnum, Lieutenant Colonel William P. Carlin, Mrs. Myles Moylan, Lieutenant Thomas W. Custer, Captain William Thompson, Lieutenant James Calhoun, Mrs. Donald McIntosh, 1st Lieutenant Myles Moylan, 2nd Lieutenant Donald McIntosh. Also published as a cabinet card (**K-122V**) by David F. Berry, recipient of Goff's original negatives in the 1880s, now in the collection of Andrew Monte.

K-122V—

K-123—Lieutenant Colonel George A. Custer and Libbie, in their study, Fort Abraham Lincoln, November 1873, by Orlando S. Goff. From the unique, original, direct-contact albumen print, courtesy of Custer Battlefield National Monument.

K-124—Lieutenant Colonel George Armstrong Custer in his study, Fort Abraham Lincoln, November 1873, by Orlando S. Goff. From the unique, original, direct-contact albumen print, courtesy of Custer Battlefield National Monument.

1874

K-125—Lieutenant Colonel George Armstrong Custer, June 1874, by photographer Huntington of Taylor's Gallery, St. Paul, Minnesota. From the unique original cabinet card, courtesy of Custer Battlefield National Monument.

K-126—Lieutenant Colonel George Armstrong Custer, June 1874, by photographer Huntington of Taylor's Gallery, St. Paul, Minnesota. Copied from the unique original, unpublished cabinet card, courtesy of the United States Army Military History Institute.

This set was possibly taken by the firm of Taylor and Huntington, who in the 1880s published original Civil War photographs from the original negatives at No. 2 Street, Hartford, Connecticut, under the management of John C. Taylor.

K-127—Custer with the first grizzly he killed, August 7, 1874, by William H. Illingworth, St. Paul, Minnesota. Identified, from left, are: Indian scout Bloody Knife, Lieutenant Colonel George A. Custer, Private Noonan, and Captain William Ludlow. From an original stereoview now in the collection of Julie Landis.

K-128—Custer with the first grizzly he killed, August 7, 1874, by William H. Illingworth, St. Paul, Minnesota. From an original contact print, from the unique, original collodian half stereoview negative courtesy of South Dakota Historical Society.

K-129—(*Overleaf*) Custer's officer and scientific corps, Black Hills Expedition, August 13, 1874, by William H. Illingworth. From an original imperial albumen print, courtesy of Dr. Lawrence A. Frost. Identified, from left, are: Captain William Ludlow, engineer officer; Captain George W. Yates, Company F, 7th U.S. Cavalry; 1st Lieutenant Thomas W. Custer, Company L, 7th U.S. Cavalry; 1st Lieutenant Donald McIntosh, Company G, 7th U.S. Cavalry (standing); 2nd Lieutenant George D. Wallace, Company G, 7th U.S. Cavalry; Captain Thomas H. French, Company M, 7th U.S. Cavalry (reclining on ground); 1st Lieutenant James Calhoun, Company C, 7th U.S. Cavalry; 2nd Lieutenant Henry M. Harrington, Company C, 7th U.S. Cavalry; 1st Lieutenant Edward G. Mathey; 1st Lieutenant Algernon Smith, quartermaster, 7th U.S. Cavalry; unknown civilian (standing); Michael Smith (standing); George Bird Grinnell, scientist (standing); Major John W. Williams, assistant surgeon; Major George A. Forsyth, 9th U.S. Cavalry, battalion commander; Lieutenant Colonel George A. Custer (reclining); A. B. Donaldson, scientist and correspondent for the *St. Paul Pioneer*; 1st Lieutenant Thomas W. McDougall, Company E, 7th U.S. Cavalry; Bloody Knife; Major Joseph E. Tilford, 7th U.S. Cavalry; Newton H. Winchell, geologist (standing); Luthor North, scientist (standing); 2nd Lieutenant Frederick D. Grant, A.D.C. (seated on ground); 2nd Lieutenant Charles A. Varnum, Company A, 7th U.S. Cavalry (reclining on ground); unidentified; Captain Myles Moylan, Company A, 7th U.S. Cavalry; 2nd Lieutenant Randall Gates, 20th U.S. Infantry; Captain Verling K. Hart, Company C, 7th U.S. Cavalry; Captain Lloyd Wheaton, Company I, 20th U.S. Infantry; unknown (standing); 2nd Lieutenant George H. Roach, Company G, 17th U.S. Infantry (standing); 1st Lieutenant Josiah Chance, 17th U.S. Infantry (standing); Louis H. Sanger, 17th U.S. Infantry (seated); Captain Owen Hale, Company K, 7th U.S. Cavalry; 2nd Lieutenant Benjamin Hodgson, Company B, 7th U.S. Cavalry (reclining); Captain Frederick W. Benteen, Company H, 7th U.S. Cavalry; 1st Lieutenant Edward S. Godfrey, Company K, 7th U.S. Cavalry; 1st Lieutenant Francis M. Gibson, Company H, 7th U.S. Cavalry. Not identified, yet probably in the picture, are: Acting Assistant Surgeon S. J. Allen and Acting Assistant Surgeon A. C. Bergen.

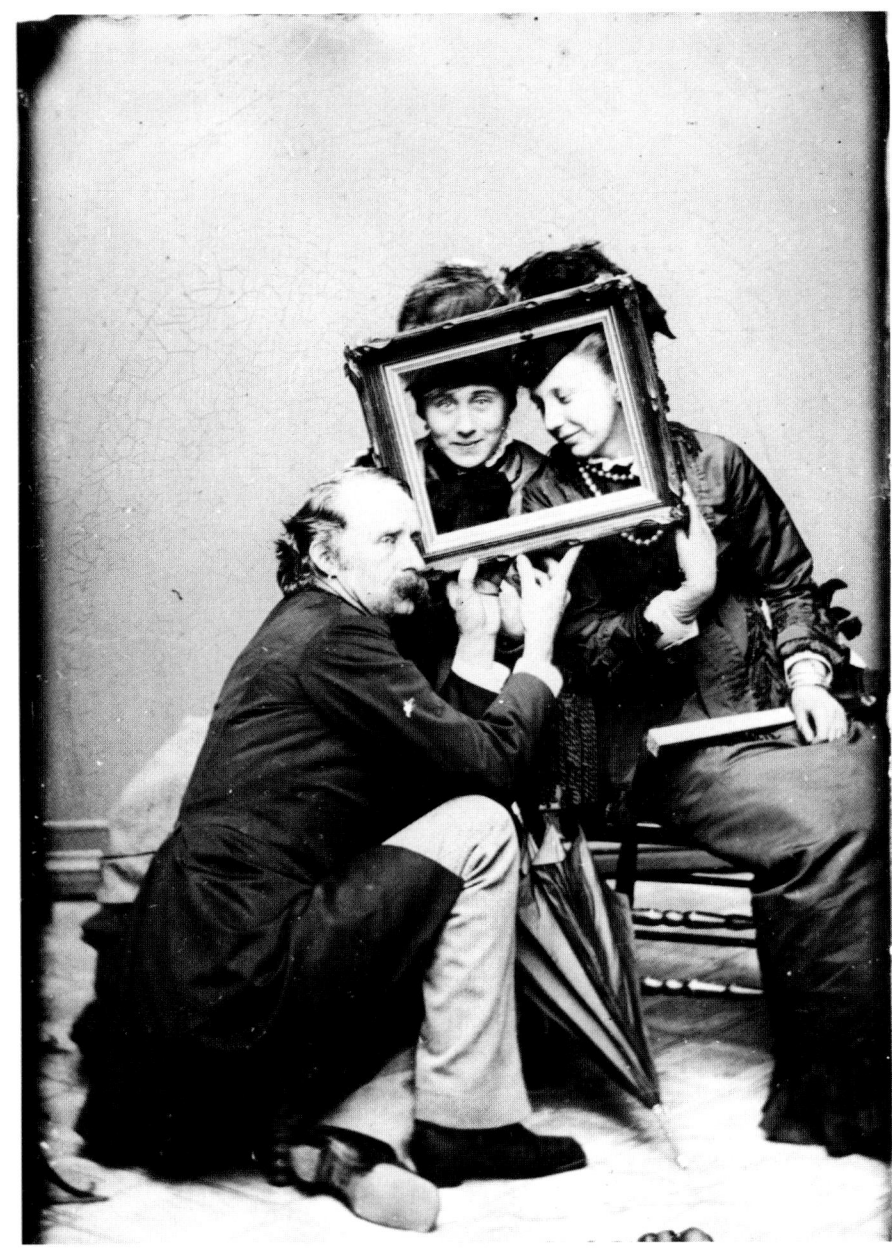

K-131—Lieutenant Colonel George A. Custer with subjects who are purported to be the Bates sisters, Agnes Bates Wellington and Nellie Bates Wadsworth. Possibly taken in November 1874, in Monroe, Michigan, by an unidentified photographer. Copied from the unique, original tintype, courtesy of Dr. Lawrence A. Frost.

K-130—Lieutenant Colonel George A. Custer with his Indian scouts, Black Hills Expedition, August 1874, by William H. Illingworth. From the unique, original, direct-contact albumen print, courtesy of Custer Battlefield National Monument. Custer is seated in the chair, and Bloody Knife is pointing to the map. The rest of the Indians are unidentified.

K-132—Lieutenant Colonel George A. Custer, November 8, 1874, by William H. Illingworth. From the unique, original, unpublished cabinet card, courtesy of Dr. Lawrence A. Frost.

1875

K-133—Lieutenant Colonel George A. Custer with three unidentified women, May 8, 1875, by Edward M. Estabrooke, New York City. From the unique, original, unpublished tintype, courtesy of Custer Battlefield National Monument.

K-134—Lieutenant Colonel George A. Custer, May 8, 1875, by Edward M. Estabrooke. From the unique, original, unpublished tintype, courtesy of Custer Battlefield National Monument.

ESTABROOKE, 31 Union Square.

K-135—Lieutenant Colonel George A. Custer, May 8, 1875, by Edward M. Estabrooke. From the unique, original, unpublished cabinet card, courtesy of Custer Battlefield National Monument.

K-136—Lieutenant Colonel George A. Custer with his sister, Mrs. Margaret Custer Calhoun, representing Quaker Peace Commissioners in a tableaux at Fort Abraham Lincoln, summer 1875, by Orlando S. Goff. From an original cabinet card, courtesy of Custer Battlefield National Monument.

K-137—Lieutenant Colonel George A. Custer and sister Margaret Calhoun, representing Quaker Peace Commissioners, and Miss Agnes Bates, representing a Sioux chief's daughter, taken during a tableaux at Fort Abraham Lincoln, summer 1875, by Orlando S. Goff. From an original cabinet card, courtesy of Custer Battlefield National Monument.

K-138—*(Left)* Lieutenant Colonel George A. Custer and Miss Agnes Bates, as a Sioux chief and his daughter, during a tableaux at Fort Abraham Lincoln, summer 1875, by Orlando S. Goff. From an original cabinet card, courtesy of Custer Battlefield National Monument.

K-139—*(Below)* Lieutenant Colonel George A. Custer and Miss Agnes Bates, as a Sioux chief and his daughter, during a tableaux at Fort Abraham Lincoln, summer 1875, by Orlando S. Goff. From an original cabinet card, courtesy of Dale Anderson.

K-140—*(Opposite)* Outing at the Little Hart River near Fort Abraham Lincoln, July 1875, by Orlando S. Goff. From an original cabinet card, courtesy of George Nas. Identified, from left, are: Lieutenant James Calhoun; Mr. Leonard Swett; Captain Stephen Baker, 6th U.S. Infantry; Boston Custer; 2nd Lieutenant Winfield S. Edgerly; Miss Emily Watson; Captain Myles W. Keogh; Mrs. Margaret Custer Calhoun; Mrs. Elizabeth B. Custer; Dr. Holmes O. Paulding; Lieutenant Colonel George A. Custer; Mrs. Nettie Smith; Dr. George E. Lord; Captain Thomas B. Weir; 1st Lieutenant William W. Cooke; 2nd Lieutenant Richard E. Thompson, 6th U.S. Infantry; Miss Nellie Wadsworth; Miss Emma Wadsworth; 1st Lieutenant Thomas W. Custer; 1st Lieutenant Algernon E. Smith.

K-141—Custer's quarters, Fort Abraham Lincoln, July 1875, by Orlando S. Goff. From an original, direct-contact albumen print, courtesy of Custer Battlefield National Monument. Identified, from left, are: Leonard Swett, W. C. Curtis, Mrs. Elizabeth B. Custer, Lieutenant James Calhoun, Miss Emma Wadsworth, Lieutenant Colonel George A. Custer, 1st Lieutenant Thomas W. Custer, Mrs. Margaret Custer Calhoun, 2nd Lieutenant Richard E. Thompson, Miss Nellie Wadsworth, and an unidentified soldier.

K-142—*(Opposite)* Custer's quarters, Fort Abraham Lincoln, July 1875, by Orlando S. Goff. From an original, direct-contact albumen print, courtesy of Custer Battlefield National Monument. Identified, from left, are: Leonard Swett, Mrs. Elizabeth B. Custer, Mrs. Margaret Custer Calhoun, Lieutenant James Calhoun, an unidentified trooper. Second row: W. C. Curtis, 2nd Lieutenant Richard E. Thompson, and Miss Emma Wadsworth. Bottom row: 1st Lieutenant Thomas W. Custer, Miss Nellie Wadsworth, and Lieutenant Colonel George A. Custer.

K-143—Custer's quarters, Fort Abraham Lincoln, July 1875, by Orlando S. Goff. Copied from an original, direct-contact albumen print, courtesy of the State Historical Society of North Dakota. Identified, from left, standing, are: Bloody Knife, Mrs. Elizabeth B. Custer, Mrs. Margaret Custer Calhoun, 1st Lieutenant Algernon E. Smith, 1st Lieutenant James Calhoun. Lower rows: 1st Lieutenant Thomas W. Custer; Mrs. Nettie Smith; Miss Emma Wadsworth; Herbert Swett; 2nd Lieutenant Richard E. Thompson; Captain Myles Keogh; Miss Nellie Wadsworth; Mrs. Myles Moylan; Boston Custer; Captain Stephen Baker, 6th U.S. Infantry; Miss Emily Watson; and Lieutenant Colonel George A. Custer.

K-144—Inside Custer's quarters, Fort Abraham Lincoln, July 1875, by Orlando S. Goff. From an original, direct-contact albumen print, courtesy of Custer Battlefield National Monument. Identified, from left, are: Boston Custer, Mrs. Margaret Custer Calhoun, 2nd Lieutenant Winfield S. Edgerly, Mrs. Elizabeth B. Custer, Mr. Leonard Swett, 2nd Lieutenant Richard E. Thompson, Miss Nellie Wadsworth, 1st Lieutenant Thomas W. Custer, Lieutenant Colonel George A. Custer, Miss Emma Wadsworth, and Miss Emily Watson.

K-145—Inside Custer's quarters, Fort Abraham Lincoln, July 1875, by Orlando S. Goff. Copied from an original, direct-contact albumen print, courtesy of State Historical Society of North Dakota. Identified, from left, are: Boston Custer, Mrs. Margaret Custer Calhoun, 2nd Lieutenant Winfield S. Edgerly, Miss Emma Wadsworth, Mrs. Elizabeth B. Custer, Mr. Leonard Swett, 2nd Lieutenant Richard E. Thompson, 1st Lieutenant Thomas W. Custer, Miss Nellie Wadsworth, Miss Emily Watson, and Lieutenant Colonel George A. Custer.

K-146—*(Opposite)* General Custer and party, along the Missouri River, summer 1875, by Orlando S. Goff. From the unique, original, direct-contact albumen print, courtesy of Custer Battlefield National Monument. Identified, from left, are: Captian William Winer Cooke, Miss Emma Wadsworth, two Indian scouts, Lieutenant Colonel George A. Custer, Miss Nellie Wadsworth, Captain Thomas W. Custer, Mrs. Elizabeth B. Custer, Mrs. George Yates, Lieutenant Winfield Scott Edgerly.

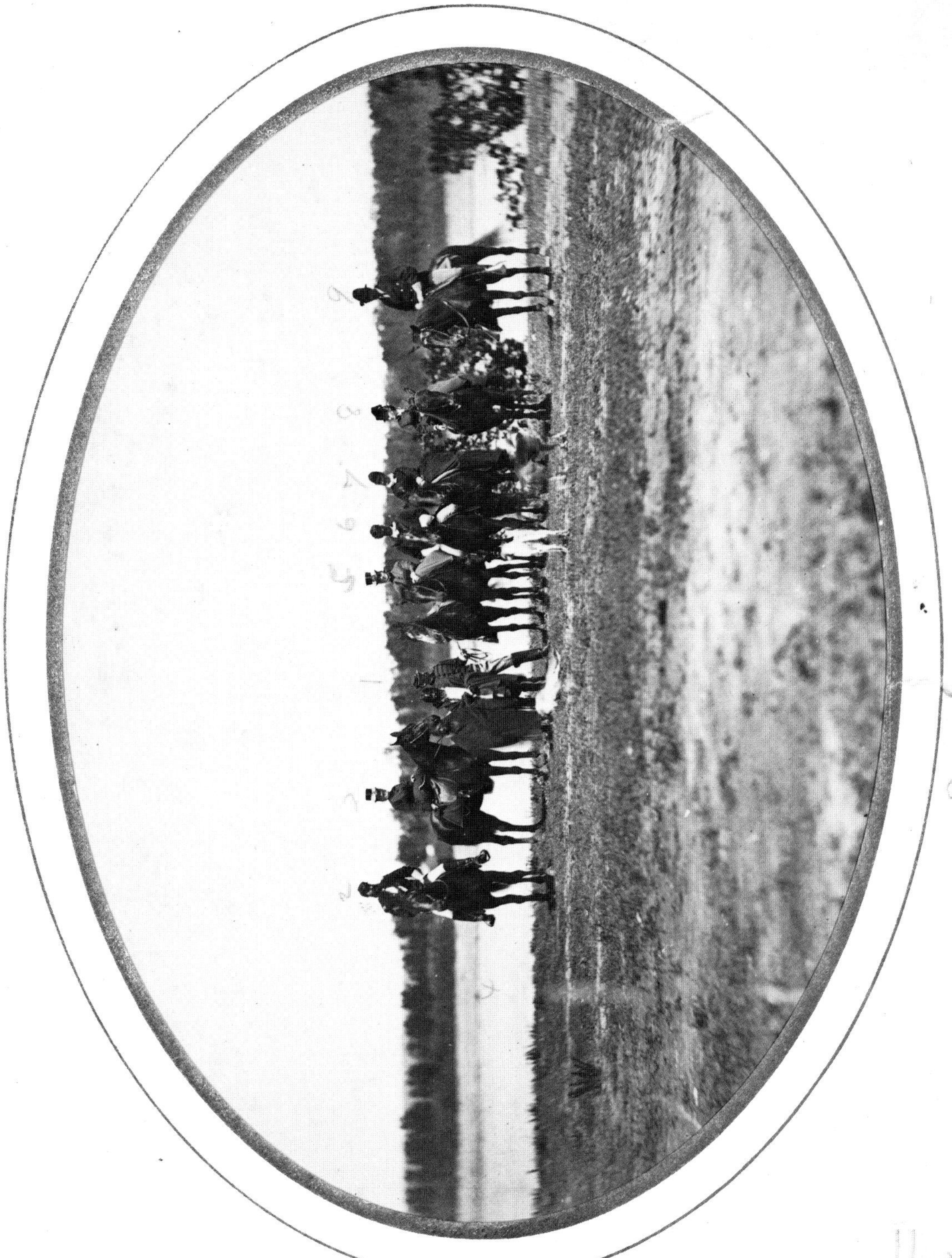

K-146—

1876

K-147V—

K-147—Lieutenant Colonel George Armstrong Custer, on or about March 1876, by José M. Mora, New York City. From an original cabinet card, courtesy of Custer Battlefield National Monument. Also published as a carte de visite (**K-147V**), now in the collection of Darryl Lyons.

K-148—Lieutenant Colonel George Armstrong Custer, on or about March 1876, by José M. Mora. Copied from the unique, original, direct-contact albumen print now lost, though once at the Sternberg Memorial Museum, Fort Hays, Kansas, courtesy of Custer Battlefield National Monument.

K-149V—

K-149—Lieutenant Colonel George Armstrong Custer, on or about March 1876, by José M. Mora. From an original, unpublished cabinet card, now in the collection of Andrew Monte. Also published as a carte de visite (K-149V), in the author's collection.

K-150V—

K-150—Lieutenant Colonel George Armstrong Custer, on or about March 1876, by José M. Mora. From an original cabinet card, now in the collection of Darryl Lyons. Also published as a carte de visite (**K-150V**), in the author's collection.

133

K-151V—

K-151—Lieutenant Colonel George Armstrong Custer, on or about March 1876, by José M. Mora. From an original cabinet card, courtesy of Andrew Monte. Also published as a carte de visite (**K-151V**), now in the collection of G. M. Brady.

K-152V—

K-152—Lieutenant Colonel George Armstrong Custer, on or about March 1876, by José M. Mora. From an original, unpublished cabinet card. Also published as a carte de visite (**K-152V**), in the author's collection.

K-153—Lieutenant Colonel George Armstrong Custer, on or about April 23, 1876, by William R. Howell. From the unique, original, unpublished carte de visite, from the lost cabinet-sized negative, now in the collection of Darryl Lyons.

K-154—Lieutenant Colonel George Armstrong Custer, on or about April 23, 1876, by William R. Howell. From the unique, original, unpublished cabinet card, courtesy of Custer Battlefield National Monument.

K-155—Lieutenant Colonel George Armstrong Custer, on or about April 23, 1876, by William R. Howell. From an original cabinet card now in the collection of Arthur Strawbridge.

K-156—General Philip Sheridan and his staff, January 2, 1865, by Alexander Gardner. From an original unpublished *carte de visite* in the author's collection. Identified from left are: Generals Wesley Merritt, James William Forsyth, George Crook, Philip H. Sheridan, and George A. Custer.

K-157—Officers and others accompanying President Andrew Johnson on his "Swing around the circle," September, 1866. Identified as follows from left, standing: Wesley Merritt, Albion P. Howe, George A. Custer. Seated: General G. K. Warren, Secretary of Navy Gideon Welles, President Andrew Johnson, Alfred Pleasonton, Secretary of State William H. Seward, General U. S. Grant, and Admiral David G. Farragut. Copied from an original unpublished albumen print courtesy of the Henry E. Huntington Library and Art Gallery.

K-158—Lieutenant Colonel George A. Custer and Spotted Tail at the Grand Duke's Mess Tent, January 1872, by D. E. Powers, employed by E. L. Eaton, Omaha, Nebraska. From the original, unpublished stereoview, courtesy of William M. Lentz, Jr.

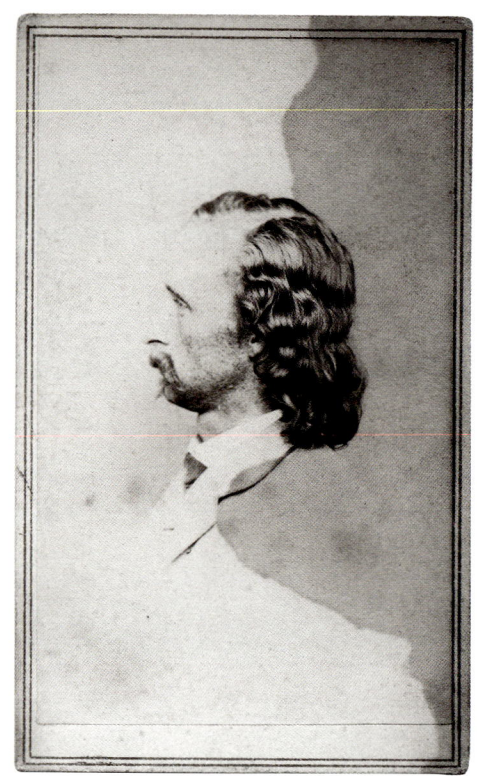

K-159-Captain George Armstrong Custer, April 1863, attributed to Henry Ulke, Washington, D.C. From the unique original unpublished carte de visite courtesy Arthur C. Unger.

K-160-Brigadier General George Armstrong Custer, November 1863 by Jno. Holyland Metropolitan Gallery, Washington, D.C. From the unique original unpublished carte de visite courtesy of Anni, Richard and Sathita Frey, now in the author's collection.

K-161-Lt. Colonel George Armstrong Custer with his wife
Elizabeth and an unidentified member of the 10th U.S. Cavalry,
September 1867, attributed to Jay Noble & Co., Ft. Leavenworth,
Kansas. From the unique original unpublished carte de visite
now in a private collection.

K-162-Lt. Colonel George Armstrong Custer George Armstrong Custer with the 7th Cavalry during
the Black Hills Expedition, on or about August 20, 1874 by William H. Illingworth, St. Paul,
Minnesota. Identified from left are Lt. Colonel George A. Custer; 1st Lt. Thomas W. Custer, Company
L; Captain Lloyd Wheaton, Company I, 20th U.S. Infantry; Captain William Ludlow, Engineer Officer,
unknown and Captain George W. Yates, Company F.

Custer Chronology

1861

June 24 — Graduates West Point.

June 29 — As Officer of the Guard, and upon his arrival at the scene of a scuffle between cadets William Ludlow and Peter M. Ryerson, Custer shouts, "Stand back boys, let's have a fair fight." As a result, Custer is arrested for conduct to the prejudice of good order.

July 5, 6 — Hearing held at West Point.

July 18 — Custer departs West Point for Washington, D.C., to join his regiment. Arrives in New York City in the early afternoon, and goes to Horstmanns and purchases his military sword, Colt side-hammer pocket pistol, and spurs. Had a quarter plate ambrotype made for his sister, Lydia (K-3).

July 20 — At the War Department, at 2 p.m., presented to General Winfield Scott. Assigned to Company G, 2nd U.S. Cavalry. Ordered to return at 8 p.m. with a horse to deliver dispatches to General McDowell at his headquarters in the field at Manassas, Virginia.

July 21 — Arrives in Manassas very early in the morning with the dispatches for General McDowell. Battle of Bull Run or Manassas. Custer leads his troops in an orderly retreat across Cub Run Bridge.

Late July, early August — Assigned to General Philip Kearny's staff.

August 3 — Ordered to Cliffburn, and the outer defenses of Washington, D.C.

October — Applies for sick leave, and departs Washington, D.C., for Monroe, Michigan.

1862

February — Returns to Washington, D.C., and its outer defenses.

March 9 — Commanding a troop of cavalry, Custer is part of a column of troops used on a reconnaisance mission to divert enemy observation.

March 14 — Custer leads a charge over Cedar Run, and drives away the Confederate pickets. One soldier and one horse are wounded; one of the early casualties of the new Army of the Potomac.

March 26 — Custer departs from Alexandria, Virginia, via steamer to Fortress Monroe.

April 4 — Custer's regiment ordered to march up the James River under General Erasmus D. Keyes.

April 7 — Along with Lieutenant Nicholas Bowen of the Topographical Engineers, Custer is assigned to the staff of General William F. (Baldy) Smith.

April 24 — Commands a company in a skirmish at New Bridge, Virginia.

May 1 — Initial ascent in a reconnaisance balloon.

May 4 — Prior to sunrise, while afloat in the balloon, Custer observes and reports to General Smith that the Confederates are evacuating toward Williamsburg.

May 5 — Leading a column, Custer extinguishes a fire to a key bridge over Skiff Creek and is cited for gallantry. Attached to General Hancock, Custer observes the Battle of Williamsburg. Custer leads a charge that results in capturing a Confederate battle flag, the first captured by the Army of the Potomac. Custer is cited for bravery, the second citation that day.

May 20 — Encamped along the Chickahominy River, Custer poses for numerous photographs along with Lieutenants Nicholas Bowen and William G. Jones. (K-4, K-5)

May 23 — Under the direction of General Barnard, Custer crosses the Chickahominy River attempting to discover a suitable ford. On the other side, Custer spies a Confederate sentry and notes his position. General McClellan requests to meet Custer, and appoints him to his staff. Custer's appointment confirmed by Secretary Stanton on June 5, with the rank of brevet captain.

May 24 — Custer accompanies Company A in its capture of the enemy sentry position discovered the day before. Fifty prisoners are taken, while Custer distinguishes himself in the fight.

May 28 — Custer is formally appointed aide de camp to General McClellan.

May 31 — Confederate courier Lieutenant James Barroll Washington, a member of General Joseph E. Johnston's staff, captured at the Battle of Fair Oaks or Seven Pines, is met by Custer at McClellan's headquarters. Custer arranged good treatment, and sat for two photographic portraits. (K-6, K-7)

June 27 — Custer leads two brigades across the grapevine bridge on the Chickahominy River, breaking through and relieving General Fitz-John Porter and the right wing of the Union army.

July 1 — Battle of Malvern Hill.

August 3 — Custer clashes with Confederate cavalry, and kills a Confederate major, claiming his famous "Toledo blade," inscribed "Draw me not without provocation. Sheathe me not without honor."

Late August — Custer visits his West Point friend, Gimlet Lea, wounded and on parole at Williamsburg, Virginia. Custer receives permission to attend the wedding of his friend to the daughter of the owner of the house in which he was staying. Custer's date was the bride's cousin, a resident of Richmond, Virginia. After the wedding, Custer learns that McClellan has moved on to Yorktown. Custer stays on in Williamsburg for almost two weeks.

September 8 — Custer reports to General McClellan at Rockville, Maryland.

September 13 — Accompanying General McClellan, Custer enters Frederick, Maryland. Lee's battle plans are discovered and Custer is ordered to accompany General Pleasonton for an attack on Turner's Gap.

September 14 — Custer and Pleasonton arrive at Turner's Gap; the Battle of South Mountain.

September 15 — Custer, along with Colonel Elon J. Farnsworth's 8th Illinois Cavalry, attacks a rear guard of Confederate skirmishers, capturing two abandoned cannons and several hundred Confederate stragglers. Custer is cited for heroism.

September 17 — During the Battle of Antietam, Custer is at the side of his commander, General McClellan.

First week of October — Custer is with General McClellan at his headquarters at Antietam.

October 3 — General McClellan meets with President Abraham Lincoln at General Fitz-John Porter's headquarters, Antietam. Custer stands off to the side and is photographed with his commander. (K-8)

November — General McClellan is relieved of command on the 7th, and Custer travels to Monroe, Michigan, on leave. Custer stops briefly at Philadelphia, and has his portrait taken by Edward K. Hipple. (K-9)

Thanksgiving — Custer is formally introduced to Elizabeth Bacon at a party given in his honor at Monroe, Michigan.

December — Custer ordered to report to General McClellan in Trenton, New Jersey, as McClellan requested his assistance in preparing his official account of the prior campaigns.

1863

January — Custer obtains a leave from General McClellan, and returns to Monroe, Michigan.

April 8 — Custer returns to General McClellan at McClellan's new home in New York City.

May 3 — Attached to General Pleasonton's command at the Battle of Chancellorsville.

May 6 — Custer is appointed aide de camp to General Alfred Pleasonton.

May 19 — Custer, representing General Pleasonton, departs on a raid under the command of Captain George H. Thompson, 3rd Indiana Cavalry, with seventy-five troopers to capture Confederate currency being transported from Richmond to Urbanna, Virginia.

May 24 — Custer returns from the Urbanna Raid, with numerous prisoners, while destroying property along the way.

Early June — While encamped at Falmouth, Virginia, Custer has his portrait made with General Pleasonton. (K-14)

June 9 — Custer, while attached to the 8th New York Cavalry, skirmishes with J. E. B. Stuart's cavalry at Beverly Ford. At Beverly Station, Lee is discovered moving north. Custer was sent to General Hooker's headquarters with a captured flag and a list of prisoners. Custer is cited for gallantry at Beverly Ford by General Pleasonton.

June 17 — Along with General Kilpatrick, Custer charges the Confederate cavalry at Aldie, Virginia.

June 19 — Custer is with Kilpatrick at Middleburg, Virginia.

June 21 — Custer is with Kilpatrick at Upperville, Virginia.

June 25 — With General Pleasonton, crosses the Potomac into Maryland.

June 26 — While stationed with General Pleasonton at Frederick, Maryland, Custer is notified of his promotion to brigadier general, U.S. Volunteers.

June 29 — Custer accepts his commission and notifies Secretary Stanton as such. He is assigned the 2nd Brigade, in Kilpatrick's 3rd Division. He enters Pennsylvania in search of General Lee.

June 30 — At Littlestown and Hanover, Pennsylvania.

July 1 — At Abbottstown and Heidlersburg, Pennsylvania, during the opening of the Battle of Gettysburg.

July 2 — While outside Hunterstown, Pennsylvania, Custer encounters Confederate cavalry. Custer charges blindly, losing 32 men and his horse, shot from beneath him. Kilpatrick orders him to march to Meade's right. Custer is cited for gallantry.

July 3 — Custer is ordered by General David McM. Gregg to return to his prior position north of the Federal line, Custer's troops are deployed along the Low Dutch Road, at the extreme right of the Federal line. At approximately 3 p.m., Custer orders his troops to first attack, then charge General J. E. B. Stuart's troops while denying them access to the Federal rear. On Custer's second attempt, the Confederate line is broken.

July 4 — Custer's brigade is led to Emmitsburg, Maryland, in pursuit of Lee's retreating army. Kilpatrick orders Custer to pursue Lee that evening across South Mountain. Custer captures Lee's train, consisting of 300 wagons, fifteen ambulances and a guard of 1,300 men outside Ringgold, Maryland.

July 5 — Custer leads his brigade through Smithsburg and Boonsboro, Maryland, finding no sign of Lee's army.

July 6 — At Williamsport, Maryland, Custer encounters a Confederate picket and attempts to destroy the bridge across the Potomac into Virginia. Kilpatrick orders Custer to withdraw his position and allow the Confederates to escape.

July 14 — Lee's rear guard finally crosses the Potomac into Virginia. At all times, Custer's brigade pounds and harasses the fleeing Confederates.

July 17 — Custer, acting as division commander during the absence of Kilpatrick, crosses the Potomac into Berlin, Virginia.

July 20 — At Ashby's Gap, Virginia, Custer skirmishes with the Confederates.

July 22 — Custer is at Upperville, Virginia.

July 23 — Custer crosses the Rappahannock into Amissville, Virginia, from where he races to Culpepper in an attempt to form a wedge between A. P. Hill and James Longstreet. Outside Orange Courthouse, Custer's brigade is met by Hill's entire corps. Unable to gather support from Meade's infantry. Custer is forced to retreat to Warrenton Junction, Virginia.

August 4 — Custer relieved from temporary command by the returning Kilpatrick.

Mid-August — Custer's brigade is ordered to re-deploy below Aquia Creek.

September 13 — General Meade orders his troops to advance, while Custer rides on the extreme left of the Union front line. During the Battle of Culpepper Courthouse, Custer leads a charge and takes J. E. B. Stuart's headquarters, and is wounded by a shell on the inside of his thigh, killing his horse. According to a surgeon's certificate, Custer is unfit for active duty. Custer leaves his command on sick leave to go to Monroe, Michigan, to petition Judge Bacon for his daughter's hand in marriage.

September 16 — Custer arrives in Monroe, Michigan.

September 28 — A masquerade party is held in honor of Custer at the Humphrey house.

October 7 — Custer arrives in Baltimore, Maryland, and catches a train to Washington, D.C. Custer goes to the theater and spends the night in D.C.

October 8 — Prior to boarding the train, Custer visits Matthew Brady's Gallery and has a series of portraits taken. (K-17—K-22)

October 9 — At General Pleasonton's headquarters in Warrenton, Virginia, Custer sits for a series of portraits in the field for the photographer Timothy H. O'Sullivan, employed by Alexander Gardner. (K-23—K-24)

October 10 — Custer breaks camp and moves against Stuart at Robertson's River.

October 11 — Custer is forced to retreat. Upon his arrival at his camp at Culpepper, he is notified that Meade has retreated past the Rappahannock. Surrounded, Custer is forced to charge the enemy line, where he cuts through and arrives at the bank of the Rappahannock at 8 p.m. Two horses are shot out from under him and he is cited for gallantry.

October 19 — At Buckland Mills, Custer's troops again capture Stuart's headquarters.

November 8 — Meade establishes winter quarters at Brandy Station, Virginia.

November 22 — Custer is at Stevensburg, Virginia.

November 6 — In an attempt to flank Lee and force him out into the open, Meade orders Custer to draw Lee out across the Rapidan.

December 7 — Custer cuts his hair short in preparation for his wedding.

December 22 — Provided with a 48-hour pass, Custer goes to Washington, D.C. He goes to Brady's Gallery and picks up the portraits made on October 8.

1864

January 26 — Custer authorized 30 days leave to return to Monroe, Michigan, and get married.

January 29 — Custer and his staff leave for Monroe, Michigan.

February 9 — Custer is married to Elizabeth Bacon at the First Presbyterian Church by the Reverend Dr. Boyd.

February 10 — Custer and Libbie depart on the midnight train and arrive at Cleveland at 9 a.m., where they stay at the Waddell House.

February 11 — Custer and Libbie headed east, traveling through Buffalo, Rochester, and Onondaga, where they visited Libbie's relations.

February 12 — Custer and his wife arrive at West Point.

February 13 — Custer and his wife depart West Point for New York City, where they stay at the Metropolitan Hotel.

February 15 — Custer and Libbie go to Matthew Brady's New York Gallery and have a series of photographs taken. (K-23—K-28)

February 17 — Custer departs New York City for Washington, D.C., where upon his arrival is ordered to immediately return to his command at Stevensburg, Virginia, five miles south of Brandy Station.

February 28 — Custer leaves on a secret raid toward Charlottesville, and camps the first evening at Madison Court House.

February 29 — Custer travels through Wolfton and Standardsville, arresting all males as potential spies or soldiers. Later that afternoon, his men capture an enemy artillery outpost and 50 prisoners.

Hearing that Fitzhugh Lee's men are at Charlottesville, Custer decides to return to Brandy Station. Bridges are burned and mills and supplies are destroyed during this retreat.

March 24 — Custer is given 20 days sick leave to recover from a concussion received in a fall from a carriage on March 14. Traveling to Washington, D.C., in the company of General Grant, Custer searches for a suitable boardinghouse for Libbie. Attending the theater, and socializing with politicians, Custer and Libbie are introduced to President Lincoln by Congressman Kellogg.

March 31 — Custer returns to his command, intending to report to his new commander, General Philip H. Sheridan.

April 4 — Custer notified that he is to assume command of the 2nd Brigade, 3rd Division, Cavalry Corps, under General Torbert.

April 23 — Custer shaves his mustache and mails it to Libbie.

May 1 — Custer provided with a 48-hour pass. In Washington, Custer visits Brady's Gallery and has two portraits taken. (K-36, K-37)

May 5 — Custer's brigade crosses the Rapidan and camps near the Wilderness.

May 6 — Custer ordered to take the Furnaces Road, east of Lee's troops to re-enforce Torbert's command. Custer's troops dismount and fight beside General John Gibbon for two days.

May 7 — Custer joins Sheridan and Gregg at Todd's Tavern, but Meade prevents them from pursuing Lee into Spotsylvania.

May 9 — Leading Sheridan's columns south, and as J. E. B. Stuart's cavalry hits the rear, Custer heads to Beaver Dam Station on the Virginia Central Railroad, capturing two trains and freeing 275 Union prisoners.

May 11 — At approximately 3 p.m., Custer charges Stuart's battery at Yellow Tavern, capturing two guns and 100 prisoners. General J. E. B. Stuart is killed by a member of Custer's command, and Custer is breveted lieutenant colonel for his actions.

May 12 — On the shore of the Chickahominy, Custer repairs a damaged bridge leading to Richmond.

May 13 — Custer reaches Haxall's Landing on the James River and joins General Benjamin Butler's army, where they are re-supplied by the navy.

May 16 — Sheridan and his cavalry return northward and meet with Grant and Meade.

May 28 — Custer's brigade re-enforces Gregg at the Battle of Haw's Shop.

June 11, 12 — Custer's brigade participates in the Battle of Trevilian Station, where he loses his personal wagon and many private possessions, including Libbie's ambrotype.

July 11 — Custer is given 20 days leave due to illness, during which he rests near Petersburg, Virginia. Libbie accompanies Congressman Kellogg and others to City Point, where she is met by Custer.

July 26 — Custer accompanies Libbie back to Washington, D.C., and stays the night.

July 28 — Custer returns to Washington, D.C., and is with Libbie.

July 30 — Custer leaves Washington and returns to his command.

August 6 — Sheridan and his staff, traveling to the Shenandoah Valley, pass through Washington. Libbie and Custer stay at the Metropolitan Hotel.

August 10 — Custer departs Washington for Harper's Ferry.

August — On the march, Custer is approached by Mrs. Lewis W. Washington, mother of Lieutenant James B. Washington. She gives Custer a button from George Washington's coat in appreciation for the kindness Custer showed her son when captured in 1862.

September 9 — Libbie comes down from Washington and stays at Harper's Ferry. At all opportunities, Custer comes to town to be with her.

September 19 — Opening the Winchester offensive, Custer's brigade charges the Confederates stationed at Opequon Creek. Custer pushes ahead and meets with General Averell's division. Custer charges the enemy's earthworks on the extreme left and causes them to disperse and flee through Front Royal. Custer's troops capture 700 men and seven battle standards. Custer is breveted colonel in the Regular Army.

September 22 — The Union cavalry is checked at Milford.

September 26 — Custer is assigned command of the 2nd Division, but never takes command.

September 30 — Custer takes command of the 3rd Cavalry Division.

October 3 — Custer ordered to burn all residences within a five-mile radius of his headquarters. Although later rescinded, many structures are destroyed in reprisal for Mosby's execution of captured Union troops.

October 6 — Sheridan's cavalry ordered to shorten their supply line.

October 9 — Custer and his division turn to meet General Rosser's Confederate cavalry, who have been harassing the rear. Custer deploys his men along Tom's Brook, goes forward, lifts his broad hat, and bows to Rosser, as if to say, "Let's have a fair fight." Custer's troops rout Rosser's cavalry in what is known as the "Woodstock Races." He captures Rosser's supply train and recovers his personal possessions, including Libbie's ambrotype. Included in the cache is a new uniform jacket of Rosser's.

October 15 — Custer and his command are on the north bank of Cedar Creek, near Middletown, Virginia.

October 19 — Early's command returns to surprise the Union left and opens the Battle of Cedar Creek. Averting a potential rout, Custer forms his brigade and leads a charge against Early's center. Custer and Merritt hold the entire force at bay, and at 4 p.m. Sheridan arrives with infantry. Custer is ordered to strike at a gap in Early's line, charges and breaks the Confederate line. Custer continues through the line and captures cannons, battle flags, caissons, and mortally wounds General Ramseur.

October 20 — Custer is ordered to proceed to Washington, D.C., with the captured battle flags to present to Secretary of War Stanton.

October 22 — Custer arrives in Washington and discovers that Libbie is in Newark, New Jersey, with friends. Custer immediately leaves Washington to meet her in New York.

October 23 — At 10 a.m. the captured battle flags are formally presented to Secretary of War Stanton. Custer is notified that he has been promoted to major general of the Volunteers for his actions at Cedar Creek.

November 15 — George, Tom and Libbie Custer are all at the mansion of Mr. and Mrs. Glass of Winchester, Virginia.

December 19 — As a diversion, Custer is sent to stir up trouble with General Early. Tom accompanies Custer for the first time. At Lacey Springs, Custer is surprised by Rosser. Wearing Rosser's captured coat, Custer fools the enemy and escapes capture. Custer's men capture 33 prisoners and two battle flags. During his absence, Libbie's father, stepmother, and cousin arrive in their camp for a visit.

December 25 — Custer and his family and staff pose for a Christmas portrait at his headquarters, near Winchester, Virginia, by Monroe photographer William H. Bowlsby. (K-45)

December 31 — Custer is appointed president of a military court which hears several important cases. Two deserters are shot for supplying information to the enemy.

1865

January 1 — At Winchester, General Sheridan and his staff give the Custers a surprise party prior to a short leave.

January 3 — Custer, Tom and Libbie, along with Mrs. Bacon and her cousin Rebecca Richmond, are in Washington, D.C.

January 4 — The party travels to New York City. Mrs. Bacon and Miss Richmond travel to Baltimore, Maryland, to visit friends.

January 25 — Custer's leave extended five days.

February 26 — Sheridan and his command are ordered to leave Winchester. Custer camps at Woodstock, Virginia.

February 27 — Custer camps at Lacey Springs, Virginia.

February 28 — Custer camps at Harrisonburg, Virginia.

March 1 — Custer camps at Staunton, Virginia.

March 2 — Custer, in the lead of the column, charges the Confederates stationed in Waynesboro, captures the town and chases the fleeing rebels in Early's command.

March 3 — The mayor of Charlottesville surrenders the city to Custer, who makes his headquarters near Monticello.

March 16 — Custer raids to within eleven miles of Richmond and skirmishes with Early and Rosser again. Custer's horse is stunned and falls on him. His men pull him safely from under the horse.

March 19 — Sheridan and Custer arrive at White House Landing, where Custer lines all seventeen battle flags they had captured along a fence railing.

March 24 — Custer leaves White House Landing.

March 26 — Custer's troops cross the James River and join Grant's army near Petersburg.

March 29 — Custer departs Petersburg and takes up a position on the extreme left of Grant's line.

March 31 — Custer is ordered to proceed immediately with two brigades to Dinwiddie Court House.

April 1 — The Battle of Five Forks.

April 3 — Custer clashes with Confederate forces at Namozine Church, where Tom captures a battle flag and fourteen prisoners.

April 5 — Custer arrives at Jetersville, a station on the Richmond and Danville Railroad.

April 6 — Custer attacks a gap in Lee's line, isolating Ewell's corps from the Army of Northern Virginia. Custer charges and destroys a large wagon train. At Saylor's Creek, Custer charges the re-formed Confederate line, which eventually breaks. Tom Custer is shot in the face while capturing another enemy standard. By evening, the entire enemy line is destroyed; Custer takes Generals Richard S. Ewell, George Washington Custis Lee, Joseph B. Kershaw, and James P. Simms prisoner. Also, seven to eight thousand men are captured, the largest group capture of any single battle during the war.

April 7 — Custer's men attack Appomattox Station, looking for and capturing four trains of Lee's supplies. He also captures twenty-five guns and secures the road to Lynchburg, Lee's only avenue of escape.

April 8 — Custer's men hold the crucial Lynchburg Road, and await re-enforcement by infantry. Unable to escape Grant's forces, Lee acknowledges his futile position this evening and concedes that surrender is his only alternative.

April 9 — The Confederate commanders discover that Custer's line as well as others have been massively re-enforced by infantry. The final chance for Confederate escape dissolves. Captain Simms of Longstreet's staff crosses the lines using a tattered white towel as a flag of truce. Custer's chief of staff, Edward W. Whitaker, returns with Captain Simms to relay Custer's demand for unconditional surrender. All parties soon meet at the McLean House in Appomattox, Virginia. Custer waits outside while the meeting takes place. At the end of the ceremony, General Sheridan presents Custer with the table upon which the surrender terms had been written. Custer leaves the area with the table over his head, and later that afternoon writes his famed congratulatory message to his troops, then visits with old West Point friends in the Confederate Army.

April 10 — Custer camps at Prospect Station. Custer is notified that Libbie is in Richmond accompanying the Joint Committee on the Conduct of the War, and that she had slept in Jefferson Davis' bed at the mansion.

April 11 — Early in the morning, Custer arrives at the Jefferson Davis Mansion and joins his wife. On this day, Custer has three tintypes taken, showing his thin and gaunt appearance. (K-63—K-65)

May 17 — General Sheridan is ordered to immediately leave Washington for his new command in Texas.

May 18 — Custer arrives in Washington, D.C., and notifies Stanton that he has just arrived in the city and disputes his date of rank as major general from acceptance on April 15, not the 30th.

May 23 — Custer rides in the Grand Review on top of a fiery race horse named Don Juan. Just prior to Custer's arrival by the reviewing stand, the horse bolts, knocking his hat off, yet he displays excellent horsemanship in controlling the horse.

May 24 — Custer, his staff, Libbie and his cook Eliza depart Washington for Texas to join the command offered by General Sheridan. Custer travels by rail to Parksburg, West Virginia. He then transfers to a luxurious river boat, traveling the Ohio and Mississippi Rivers to New Orleans.

June 18 — Custer and his party arrive in New Orleans.

Late June — Custer and his party arrive in Alexandria, Louisiana.

July 17 — Custer formally presented the command of the Cavalry Division of the Military District of the Southwest.

July 28 — According to Special Order #130, Custer is ordered to proceed to Hempstead, Texas, and report to Major General Wright. At about this time, Custer cuts his hair short for his comfort in the warm climate.

August — Custer is at Hempstead, Texas, on the Brenham-Galveston railway. Custer's brother Tom and father Emanuel arrive by boat from Galveston. Tom is Custer's aide, and his father is his forage agent.

November 13 — Custer and his party depart Hempstead for Austin, Texas.

November 23 — Custer and his party arrive in Austin, establishing his headquarters at the Blind Asylum.

December 15 — Custer and his wife visit San Antonio, Texas.

1866

January 31 — While in Austin, Custer receives word that his volunteer commission has expired, and he has been reduced in rank to captain in the 5th U. S. Cavalry, stationed in the East.

February 13 — Custer is in Galveston, Texas.

February 20 — Custer is in New Orleans.

March — Libbie returns to Monroe, Michigan, and Custer travels to Washington to meet with Secretary of War Stanton. Custer secures commissions in the Regular Army for Tom and George W. Yates.

March 26 — While in Washington, Custer attends a dinner party for Chief Justice Salmon Chase. Senator Chandler takes him home to visit his family. Custer is asked to appear before the Joint Reconstruction Committee about conditions in Texas.

April 28 — Custer's application for 30 days leave is approved.

May 1 — Custer travels to New York City to find employment. He visits Wall Street and the Broker's Board, which gives him three cheers. At the Manhattan Club, Custer dines with General Pleasonton and meets many West Point classmates.

May 18 — Custer is notified that Judge Bacon has died and immediately returns to Monroe, Michigan.

June — Custer, accompanied by Libbie, returns to Washington, seeking employment.

July 6 — Custer applies for the newly formed position of Inspector General of the United States Cavalry.

July 28 — Custer is offered a commission as lieutenant colonel in the newly formed 7th U. S. Cavalry. He accepts the position with the hope of finding something better in the future.

August 9 — In Detroit, Michigan, Custer attends a mass meeting to endorse the National Union Platform and is appointed one of four delegates to the national convention.

August 14 — Custer attends the national convention in Philadelphia.

August 20 — Along with five others, Custer signs a petition to call on all former soldiers and sailors to attend a grand rally for the National Union Party.

August 22 — President Andrew Johnson invites Custer and Libbie to accompany him and a presidential party to bring his policies directly to the American people. Custer accepts his offer.

September 1—Custer and Libbie join the presidential party at Manhattanville, New York, where a steamboat takes them to West Point. Secretary of State Seward, Gideon Welles, Admiral Farragut, Generals Grant, Merritt and Pleasonton accompany them on the trip.

September 3—At Niagara Falls, General Thomas joins the party, and that evening a public reception is held.

September 4 — The presidential party heads westward to Buffalo, New York; Erie, Pennsylvania; Cleveland, Ohio; and Detroit, Michigan.

September 5 — As a special trip, the train is backed into Monroe, Michigan.

September 7 — In Chicago, Illinois, Custer writes a note to the Detroit Free Press stating that he would not accept the nomination as Congressman from Michigan, yet he still endorses the National Union Platform.

September 8 — In Springfield, Illinois, the presidential party visits Lincoln's tomb.

September 9 — At St. Louis, Johnson is heckled.

September 10 — The party makes its way back to Washington, D.C. At Terre Haute, Indiana, a mob attempts to derail the train. In Indianapolis, a torchlight procession ends in riot, where one man is shot and killed. In his attempt to make a speech, Johnson is shouted down: "Shoot the damned traitor." Grant takes the platform and shouts, "For the credit of your city, hear us speak."

September 11 — The presidential party is in Louisville, Kentucky.

September 12 — In the evening, they board a steamboat for Cincinnati, Ohio.

September 13 — In Cincinnati, the presidential party visits the Spencer House, where Grant's father and Sherman's father-in-law, Thomas Ewing, wait in the reception committee.

September 14 — The train is scheduled to stop at Scio, Ohio, the nearest stop to Custer's birthplace. Hearing ugly remarks about Johnson, loud enough for Johnson to hear them, compels Custer to face the mob and shout, "I was born two miles from here, and I am ashamed of you." With that, he boards the train, signals the conductor to depart, and vows never to return there again. The Custers depart the train at Stubenville, Ohio, and return to Monroe, Michigan.

September 17 — Custer attends the Soldiers and Sailors Convention at Cleveland.

September 24 — Custer is granted an additional leave of absence.

October — The Custers, along with their friend Diana and their cook Eliza, leave for Fort Riley, Kansas. Enroute, they stop in St. Louis for one last fling.

November — The Custer party arrives at Fort Riley.

December 5 — According to the surgeon's report on a physical examination, Custer is "physically competent to perform the duties of a cavalry officer."

1867

March 1 — General Hancock's expedition departs Fort Leavenworth, Kansas, picking up the 7th Cavalry at Fort Riley. Wild Bill Hickok accompanies the expedition as a scout. Custer's promotion to lieutenant colonel is confirmed.

April 3-7 — Custer is at Fort Larned.

May 3 — Custer arrives at Fort Hays, Kansas, and reports to General Hancock.

June 1 — Custer, along with a column of 350 infantry, 20 wagons, and the 7th Cavalry, departs Fort Hays in search of renegade Indians. His orders are to scout the country between Forts Hays and McPherson, move southward to the headwaters of the Republican River, touch the Platte River at Fort Sedgwick, where he would be re-supplied; move southward to Fort Wallace on the Smokey Hill River, and return to Fort Hays.

June 6 — Custer is at White Horse Creek.

June 8 — Custer is at Medicine Creek. Major Wyckliffe Cooper commits suicide. Cooper, thought to be an enemy of Custer's, was reportedly drunk and despondent at not being with his wife, who was expecting a child.

July 7 — Fifteen men desert at 5 p.m. in full view of the entire camp. Custer gives the command to pursue the deserters and to bring the dead bodies of as many as possible back to camp. Two men are shot, one of whom later dies from his wounds.

July 10, 11 — Custer is at Fort McPherson.

July 12 — Custer leads a forced march to Fort Wallace. Arriving at Fort Wallace, Custer discovers the area is in a poor state of affairs. He decides to push on to Fort Harker, through Fort Hays, to obtain additional supplies. One hundred men are chosen for the march. Most of the troops are left at Fort Hays. Custer, Tom, Lieutenant Cooke and two troopers continue on to Fort Harker. At Fort Harker, the supplies are requisitioned, and Custer reports by wire to General Sherman.

July 16 — At Downer's Station, Custer is notified that two stragglers have been killed by Indians.

July 17 — Custer returns to Fort Hays, where it is discovered that the supplies are inadequate.

July 18 — Armstrong, Tom, Cooke and the two privates arrive at Fort Harker. Custer reports to Colonel Smith, waking him, and receives Smith's approval to continue on to Fort Riley. Later, Smith has second thoughts and orders Custer's arrest. Just before noon, Custer arrives at Fort Riley and is united with his wife.

July 21 — Custer returns to Fort Harker and is arrested. The charges against him are as follows: Leaving Fort Wallace without permission; excessive cruelty and illegal conduct in shooting deserters; abandoning two soldiers killed by Indians at Downer's Station; and marching men excessively.

August — Custer selects Captain Parsons to represent him at his trial.

September 16 — Custer's trial opens at Fort Leavenworth, Kansas.

October 12 — Custer's court martial/trial ends.

November 20 — Custer is found guilty of all charges specified. He is suspended from service and rank, with a loss of pay for one year. The Custers are staying at the quarters of General Sheridan at Fort Leavenworth.

December — Shortly after the determination of sentence, Custer and Libbie depart Kansas and return to Monroe, Michigan.

1868

September 24 — Custer is notified by General Sheridan that his services are needed and that his sentence is remitted. Custer is on the next train back to his command at Fort Hays.

October 4 — Custer arrives at Fort Hays, where he is met by General Sheridan. His troops are currently stationed at Fort Dodge.

October 18 — Custer is at Fort Dodge, Kansas.

November 12 — Custer departs Fort Dodge to establish Camp Supply.

November 18 — Custer arrives at Wolf and Beaver Creek.

November 22 — Custer receives orders for moving toward the Indian village. This signals the beginning of Custer's first major winter Indian campaign.

November 26 — The command strikes an Indian trail near the point where the Texas boundry line crosses the Canadian River. Intense reconnaisance follows and the command deploys for attack the following morning.

November 27 — At dawn, Custer divides his command into four separate columns, and charges the surprised village, located on the Washita River, Indian Territory (Oklahoma). The conflict ends after several hours, and Black Kettle's entire village of 51 lodges (Cheyenne, Arapaho, and Sioux) is destroyed. The Indians leave on the ground 103 killed, and further lose their horse herd of 875 animals, all destroyed, along with everything they possessed. Fifty-three prisoners are taken. In the 7th Cavalry, two officers and 19 enlisted men are killed; one officer is seriously wounded. Of those dead, several are with Major Elliott, who is missing in action and not accounted for until days later. Immediately after the battle, Custer discovers that the village he has just attacked is part of a much larger encampment extending at least 12 miles farther down the river valley, and that the now-enraged inhabitants of this encampment outnumber his force three to one. As the Indian forces begin to assemble, Custer determines that a daring bluff is his only chance for escape. He therefore orders the band to play, and his troops to march straight toward the assembling horde. As soon as dark overtakes the field, he reverses his march, and escapes from the area.

December 2 — Custer and his command return to Camp Supply.

December 10 — Custer and Sheridan and their command return to the Washita battlefield, where they discover the bodies of Major Elliott and his men, badly mutilated.

December 26 — Custer dines with General Sheridan at Fort Cobb Indian Reservation.

1869

January 14 — Custer leads a small expedition after renegade Indians.

Custer and his party are evaded by the Cheyennes and Kiowas, who are known to have white prisoners. Custer and his party almost starve, and at one point are forced to eat horse meat.

February 9 — Custer, wearing a beard and buckskins, poses for a tintype photographer and sends the print to Libbie as an anniversary gift. The Custer party is at Fort Sill, in the Wichita Mountains. (K-93)

April 7 — Custer is offered leave for as long as he pleases by General Sheridan, who is in Chicago. Custer decides to stay at his summer camp on Big Creek, below Fort Hays, Kansas.

Custer travels to Fort Leavenworth to bring Libbie back to his summer camp. Custer receives 200 visitors between June 1 and October 16, 1869.

June 29 — Bored with inactivity, Custer applies for the position of commandant of West Point.

September — Custer and his party are photographed by W. J. Phillips of Preston, Missouri, who accompanies them on a buffalo hunt. Lords Waterpark and Paget also accompany them on the trip. (K-99, K-100)

October 8-10 — Custer takes K. C. Baker on a buffalo hunt.

October 13 — Custer departs his camp on the Big Creek, and moves to his winter quarters at Fort Leavenworth.

November — Custer leaves Fort Leavenworth alone, and stops in Chicago to visit with General Sheridan. While in Detroit, Custer attends a reception at the Biddle House.

December 2 — Custer is in Chicago, Illinois.

December 15 — Custer is in Monroe, Michigan, to settle some matters in Judge Bacon's estate.

December 17 — Custer stops in New York.

December 18 — Custer is in Washington, D.C., and is questioned by the War Department about re-organizing the army.

December 26 — Custer and Lieutenant William W. Cooke and Mr. Barker, ex-mayor of Detroit, arrive in Hamilton, Ontario, Canada, to visit with Cooke's family at the residence of John Winer, Cooke's uncle.

December 28 — Custer posed for a series of photographs with Cooke and Mr. Barker (not located). Custer spent the remainder of the day with inventor Alexander Graham Bell.

December 29 — Custer and Cooke spent the day duck hunting at Coote's Paradise.

December 30 — Custer and Cooke depart Hamilton and head west for Monroe and the New Year, 1870.

1870

January 9 — Custer departs Washington, D.C., for Fort Leavenworth, Kansas.
Summer — Custer and Libbie return to their camp at Fort Hays, Kansas, entertaining Easterners.
July 5-8 — Custer and his party go on a grand buffalo hunt to the Saline River.
August 15 — By special invitation of the president of the Kansas-Pacific Railway, Custer is a member of an excursion trip from the Missouri River to Denver, Colorado.
August 30 — Custer is in St. Louis and Chicago.
September 10 — Custer is given thirty days leave.
October — Custer is with his regiment at Fort Leavenworth, Kansas.

1871

January 11 — Custer is given 120 days leave to consider resigning from the Army. Custer and Libbie return to Monroe, Michigan. From there, Custer travels to New York to investigate a financial career.
February — Custer is in New York, hoping to sell some mining stock.
Summer — Custer travels between Monroe, Michigan, and New York City.
July — While in New York and Saratoga, Custer asks for and receives a 30-day extension on his leave.
July 4 — Custer is in Monroe, Michigan, for a reunion of the veterans of the War of 1812. (K-104)
September 3 — Custer is ordered to report to his new post at Elizabethtown, Kentucky.
November 20 — Custer and Libbie are in Lexington, Kentucky. For two weeks, they visit in Louisville and Cincinnati, Ohio.

1872

January — Custer is ordered by General Sheridan to accompany the Grand Duke of Russia, Alexis, on a grand tour of the west and a buffalo hunt guided by Buffalo Bill Cody. The trip is provided as a good-will gesture following the United States' purchase of Alaska from Russia. The hunting party detrains at North Platte, Nebraska.
January 14 — The tour begins, passing through Denver and Topeka, Kansas, stopping at Fort Wallace and Fort Hays. (K-106, K-107)
January 24 — The hunting party is in St. Louis, Missouri. (K-108—K-112)
February — The hunting party continues to Louisville, Kentucky; Memphis, Tennessee; and New Orleans, Louisiana.
March 7 — Custer and Libbie attend the marriage of Custer's sister, Margaret, to Lieutenant James Calhoun in Monroe, Michigan. After the ceremony, they return to his command at Elizabethtown, Kentucky.
May 22 — Custer is made a member of the board to inspect cavalry horses, and is on detached service at the headquarters, Department of the South.
July 4 — Custer attends the reunion of the veterans of the War of 1812 in Monroe, Michigan.

1873

February — Custer receives orders to reunite the 7th Cavalry, now stationed at various posts, and take it to the Dakota Territory. The Northern Pacific Railroad is being constructed through hostile Sioux territory, and its construction and survey crews need constant army protection.
End of March — Custer's command assembles at Memphis, Tennessee, where three steamboats will take them on the first leg of their journey. (K-114, K-115)
April — Custer and his command leave Memphis, enroute to their command at Fort Rice, Dakota Territory.
April 10 — Custer's command commences a 350-mile march up the Missouri River, covering the final distance to Fort Rice.
June 10 — Custer's command arrives at Fort Rice. Custer reports to his commander, General David S. Stanley.
June 20 — Custer and his command leave Fort Rice and begin the Yellowstone Expedition. The Northern Pacific Railroad survey team is commanded by Custer's old friend, Confederate General Thomas L. Rosser.
June 26 — Custer and his command are on the Heart River, Dakota Territory.
July 1 — Custer is placed temporarily under arrest by General Stanley.
July 19 — Custer and his command reach the Yellowstone River, Montana Territory.
July 31 — Custer camps north of the mouth of the Powder River.
August 4 — Custer, with Companies A and B, are attacked by a force of from 250 to 300 Indians. Custer deploys his men on foot to fight the attackers. Soon they are re-enforced by the remaining troops and infantry.
August 5-7 — Custer's men are watched by the Indians from the bluffs.
August 8 — At the mouth of the Rosebud River, a large Indian village flees, with Custer's men in pursuit.
August 10 — Custer's command follows the Indians, who cross the Yellowstone River below the mouth of the Little Big Horn.
August 11 — Custer's men are surrounded by Indians across the river and behind them from the

bluffs, 600 feet to the rear. Custer's command drives them from the field.

September 6 — Custer kills the "King of the Forest," a large bull elk weighing over 300 pounds. He is photographed with it by William R. Pywell, photographer for the expedition. (K-116)

September 23 — Custer and his command return to their new post at Fort Abraham Lincoln. Immediately upon his return, Custer leaves for Monroe, Michigan.

October — Custer is in Monroe, Michigan, preparing to return with his family.

November — Custer, his wife, and Miss Agnes Bates return to their new home at Fort Abraham Lincoln.

1874

February — Custer's home at Fort Abraham Lincoln burns to the ground.

May 14 — Custer is in St. Paul, Minnesota.

July 2 — The Black Hills Expedition departs Fort Abraham Lincoln. Included are 10 troops of 7th Cavalry, two companies of infantry, and William H. Illingworth, photographer for the expedition.

July 15 — Custer's command is at Prospect Valley, Dakota Territory, 12 miles from the Montana line.

July 20 — Custer's column enters the Black Hills.

August 3 — Custer sends scout Charlie Reynolds with dispatches, across 75 miles of Indian-held plains to Fort Laramie, on the Platte in Wyoming.

August 7 — Custer kills his first grizzly bear. He poses for two photographs with William Ludlow, his chief engineer, and his Indian scout, Bloody Knife. (K-125, K-126)

August 30 — Custer and his command return to Fort Abraham Lincoln from the Black Hills Expedition.

October 20 — Custer and Libbie attend the wedding of Frederick Dent Grant in Chicago, Illinois.

November — Custer and Libbie stop at Monroe, Michigan, and pick up Armstrong's niece, Maria Reed, to return to Fort Abraham Lincoln.

November 8 — Custer and Libbie are in St. Paul, Minnesota, where a grand piano is rented for their quarters.

November 15 — The Custers return to Fort Abraham Lincoln.

December — The Custers entertain all winter, putting on small productions and plays, singing around the new grand piano.

1875

January — "Lonesome" Charlie Reynolds reports to Custer that at the Standing Rock Agency he had heard an Indian named Rain-in-the-Face boast of killing Dr. Holzinger and Mr. Balarian during the Yellowstone Expedition of 1873. Custer orders Captain Yates and Tom Custer to take 100 men and arrest the murderer. Rain-in-the-Face is captured, but escapes after months of imprisonment.

Spring — Custer goes to Bismark, North Dakota, to arrest grain thieves.

Late Summer — Secretary of War Belknap visits Fort Abraham Lincoln and is snubbed by Custer. Custer assumes that Belknap is at the root of corruption in the War Department.

September 24 — Custer, Tom and Libbie leave Fort Abraham Lincoln on a holiday to New York City.

November — Tom returns to Fort Abraham Lincoln, while Custer applies for an extension to his leave.

December — The Custers are staying at the Hotel Brunswick, New York City.

1876

January — Custer asks for and is granted another extension to his leave. They are forced to leave the Hotel Brunswick because they are low on funds.

February 5 — Custer applies for another extension of leave, but is denied.

February 15 — The Custers depart New York for his command at Fort Abraham Lincoln.

March 11 — At Fort Abraham Lincoln, Custer is notified by telegraph that he is called to Washington, D.C., to testify before the Senate committee investigating alleged corruption in the War Department.

March 12 — Custer and Libbie are snowbound in St. Paul, Minnesota; brother Tom comes to their rescue and removes them from the train.

March 14 — Custer leaves Fort Abraham Lincoln to return to Washington, D.C., to testify before the Senate committee.

March 20 — Enroute to Washington, D.C., Custer stops in New York to see his publisher and discuss the forthcoming publication of his memoirs.

March 31 — In Washington, D.C., Custer awaits his call to testify in the Clymer Investigation of Secretary Belknap. Custer denies making accusations in print that Belknap is guilty of selling army post traderships in Dakota.

April 17 — The Belknap impeachment hearings begin. Custer's statements linking Grant's brother with Belknap and others are ruled inadmissible. President Grant is incensed with Custer's damaging statements from the investigation.

April 27 — Custer is in Washington, and attempts three times to have a personal interview with President Grant. Custer wants to remove certain unjust impressions concerning his role in the investigation. President Grant refuses to see or acknowledge Custer.

May 1 — Custer leaves Washington to return to his command.

May 4 — Upon his arrival in Chicago, an aide to General Sheridan informs Custer that Sherman has ordered his arrest for leaving Washington without permission. Grant is seen as directing his arrest.

May 6 — Custer, agonizing over the distinct possibility of missing his summer expedition against the Indians, writes a pleading letter to President Grant. "I appeal to you as a soldier to spare me the humiliation of seeing my regiment march to meet the enemy, and I to not share its dangers."

May 7 — Custer leaves for St. Paul, where he awaits Grant's verdict. The request is endorsed by both General Sheridan and General Terry. General Sherman will allow Custer to join his command, yet not accompany it during the expedition.

May 8 — Custer is informed that President Grant has removed his objection and will allow him to accompany his command. Custer returns to Fort Abraham Lincoln on the train with General Terry.

May 17 — Custer and his command depart Fort Abraham Lincoln. Custer's hair at this time is short, and he wears a red tie, broad-brimmed white hat, and a fringed buckskin shirt.

June 3 — A group of scouts brings word to General Terry and Custer that General Gibbon's column has left its position near the mouth of the Rosebud on May 23.

June 9 — Custer is 20 miles from the mouth of the Powder River, Montana Territory.

June 11 — Custer is at the mouth of the Powder River.

June 15, 16 — Custer is at the mouth of the Tongue River.

June 19 — Custer receives word from Reno that he has sighted Indian trails pointing to the Little Big Horn River.

June 21 — Custer meets with Generals Terry and Gibbon on the steamer *Far West*. Custer is to follow the main trail of the Sioux, and attempt to discover their main village. Gibbon and Terry are to converge from other routes and block their escape. Custer is to meet them on June 26. Reno's estimate of the number of Indians, based on trail size is 800, but Terry figures on 1,500 braves.

June 22 — Custer receives his final written instructions from General Terry. At noon, Terry reviews Custer's troops. Shortly thereafter, the 7th Cavalry begins its march. At 4 p.m., the command camps in a deep and narrow valley of the Rosebud, junctured by the Yellowstone.

June 23 — Custer's command marches 23 miles up the Rosebud, following an ever-increasing and very large Indian trail, estimated now to contain 1,500 lodges.

June 24 — After a long, hard march, it becomes apparent that the Indians are aware of his presence. By evening, the column bivouacks approximately 25 miles east of the Little Big Horn Valley. Near 9 p.m., returning scouts inform Custer that the Indian trail leads across the divide. Custer orders the march to continue through the night.

June 25 — At dawn, Lieutenant Varnum and his Indian scouts, who are located on a high promontory called the "Crow's Nest," observe the Sioux camp and its large horse herds 15 miles to the west. They report this discovery to Custer, and note that several Sioux had been observing the cavalry column.

At 12:07 p.m., Custer halts the colunm and divides the regiment into three columns. Major Reno is assigned Companies A, G, and M. Captain Benteen is given Companies D, H, and K. Custer retains Companies C, E, F, I, and L. Company B guards the pack trains. Benteen is ordered to scout the ridges to the left. Reno and Custer continue the march in parallel columns for another nine miles, until within three miles of the river, where the Indians are fully visible and in apparent retreat. Reno is ordered to follow and charge where deemed prudent, to be supported by the whole outfit. Reno crosses the Little Big Horn River and engages the Indians, and is rapidly pushed back to the line of bluffs on the east side of the river. As this occurs, Custer continues up the east side of the Little Big Horn, roughly three miles beyond Reno, and is fully engaged by overwhelming forces. His entire command is slain. Indian forces, after defeating Custer's column, turn and surround Reno's defensive position, re-enforced by Benteen's column. Reno and Benteen are pinned down.

June 26 — Indian attacks begin again at dawn on the Reno-Benteen position. After a heavy battle, the Indian firing slacks off by noon. Evening sees the vast Indian village break up and rapidly draw off.

June 27 — Gibbon's column arrives on the battlefield at dawn. Lieutenant James H. Bradley, commander of Gibbon's scouts, finds all that remains of Custer's command. Lieutenant James Calhoun's body is found behind his men in a skirmish formation. Tom Custer lies face down, terribly mutilated, scalped several times, his skull crushed and body pierced with many arrows. His heart had been cut out. Custer's naked body is found on the highest point of the field, sitting between two soldiers, with his hand resting on the top of one. His face lies in the palm of his hand. Two wounds are obvious — a bullet hole in the left breast and one in the left temple.

NATIONAL ARCHIVES / LIBRARY OF CONGRESS
IDENTIFICATION NUMBERS

IDENTIFICATION NUMBERS:	*NEGATIVE NUMBERS:*
K-6	LC-B815-428
K-14	LC-B8171-7551
K-17	NA B-4169
K-18	NA B-4166
K-19	NA B-1922
K-22	NA B-1924
K-30	NA B-6074
K-32	LC-BH 831-702
K-33	NA B-3854
K-36	NA B-3914
K-37	NA B-3914
K-43	NA B-1801
K-44	LC-BH 831-578
K-49	NA B-1923
K-51	LC-BH 82-2268
K-53	LC-BH 831-741
K-54	NA B-4162
K-56	NA B-4889
K-57	NA B-1881
K-60	NA B-2495
K-61	NA B-1151
K-62	NA B-4509
K-62	LC-USZ 62-63839
K-72	NA B-5931
K-73	NA B-4989
K-74	NA B-5902
K-75	NA B-2193
K-76	LC-BH 831-1314
K-78	NA B-4990
K-79	LC-BH 831-365
K-104	LC-BH 832-932
K-105	LC-BH 832-29187
K-114	LC-USZ 62-42305
K-140	NA 111-SC-83991

K-147VV-This image is the most perplexing I have seen. The author believes it to be the same as K-147V. The publisher believes it to be a new photograph. There is a difference in the positioning of the tie and jacket. When a copy is lined up with K-147V, the face is identical, but the tie and jacket DO NOT line up. There is no explanation for this one, what do you think? Courtesy of Arthur C. Unger.